Rethinking Race

Rethinking Race:

A critique of contemporary
anti-racism programmes

Joanna Williams

CIVITAS

First published
April 2021

© Civitas 2021

55 Tufton Street
London SW1P 3QL

email: books@civitas.org.uk

ISBN 978-1-912581-23-8

Typeset by Typetechnique

Printed in Great Britain
by 4edge Limited, Essex

Contents

Author

Joanna Williams is director of the Freedom, Democracy and Victimhood Project at Civitas. Previously she taught at the University of Kent where she was Director of the Centre for the Study of Higher Education. Joanna is the author of *Women vs Feminism* (2017); *Academic Freedom in an Age of Conformity* (2016) and *Consuming Higher Education, Why Learning Can't Be Bought* (2012). She co-edited *Why Academic Freedom Matters* (2017) and has written numerous academic journal articles and book chapters exploring the marketization of higher education, the student as consumer and education as a public good. In addition, Joanna has written about education, feminism and gender for many popular outlets including the *The Spectator, The Sun, The Telegraph* and *American Conservative*. Joanna is a regular columnist for the online magazine *Spiked*.

Summary

By almost all statistical measures, society is less racist today than at any other point in the past century. But this is rarely celebrated. Still less is it considered a reason to leave people to negotiate inter-cultural and inter-racial relationships for themselves. Despite there being less racism today, rarely has there been more discussion about racism. The message from the media and best-selling books, as well as from an array of diversity workshops held in schools, universities and the workplace, is that not being racist is no longer sufficient: we must all be actively anti-racist. What's more, we must demonstrate our anti-racism in ways approved by a cohort of race experts.

Critical Race Theory (CRT), newly migrated from academia, provides the theoretical underpinnings for today's anti-racism industry. New phrases have entered our vocabulary: terms like systemic racism, unconscious bias, white privilege, cultural appropriation, reparations, microaggression and intersectionality, now pepper newspapers, radio discussions, charity campaigns and school lessons. Anti-racism training has become a big business with the most popular speakers and authors generating considerable revenue. But what if this ubiquitous anti-racism does little to improve outcomes for members of the BAME community? Worse, what if contemporary anti-racism breathes new life back into racial thinking and emphasises differences between people that were only recently being overcome?

This report is in two parts. Chapter one considers changing ideas around race, racism and anti-racism. Chapter two examines today's anti-racism industry from its ideological underpinnings to the specific practices enacted in the most common forms of training programmes. It draws upon a wide range of academic and popular literature, as well as interviews with participants in workplace diversity training programmes and online content from training providers. To protect interviewees, all names and other identifying features have been changed or removed. It is worth noting that even with this protection in place, many potential participants were too anxious to share their experiences for fear of losing their job if discovered.

The argument throughout is that as anti-racism has rejected the civil rights era aspiration for colour blindness, people are once more being taught to see each other as racialised beings. White people are assumed to be the beneficiaries of white privilege and black people the victims of systemic racism. Such gross racial generalisations are to the detriment of everyone in society. They call into question individual agency and attach limits on personal ambition while shoring up a grievance culture. The sole beneficiaries of this approach are elite race experts who find themselves in a powerful position to intervene in all aspects of our public and private lives.

Recommendations

1. Education and training are two distinct things. No school pupil or university student should be taught CRT as fact, have to undergo mandatory unconscious bias training, or be compelled to attend any other form of anti-racism training.

2. No employee should face losing their job for refusing to undertake workplace anti-racism training or for raising legitimate concerns with the content of such training programmes.

3. An inquiry should be held into the soliciting, investigating and recording of non-crime hate incidents. The gathering of statistics relating to such incidents has become open to exploitation by activists. Data is used to legitimise a sense of victimhood among minority communities and lend weight to the concept of microaggression.

4. Reassert the importance of equality before the law. Workplace training sessions could play a useful role in informing employees about legal duties not to discriminate.

5. Positive discrimination should be exceptional and only take place under specific and limited circumstances. In such instances where positive discrimination is deemed necessary, a candidate's social class background should be considered alongside race and sex.

6. Schools, universities and workplaces should be encouraged to place greater value upon viewpoint diversity, rather than just biological diversity, and what people have in common, rather than simply what divides us.

1.

Race, Racism and Anti-Racism Today

Black Lives Matter

In the summer of 2020, following the death of George Floyd at the hands of a Minneapolis Police Officer, Black Lives Matter (BLM) protests swept the globe. Neither police brutality towards black people nor mass demonstrations against racism are new. But rarely have people on every continent, in countries and towns facing their own unique problems, turned out in such huge numbers to support the same cause. This wave of protests took place even though the world was in the grip of the coronavirus pandemic and, in most countries, legal restrictions limited the number of people able to gather. BLM protests not only breached national lockdowns, but they also often took place with minimal law enforcement or even police backing. In the UK, some police officers went so far as to 'take the knee' before protesters.[1]

BLM is further distinct from previous protest movements in the high profile support it has received. It has been publicly endorsed by former members of the royal family and celebrities who 'blacked out' their social media profiles for a day.[2] Following the initial wave of demonstrations, sports stars wore kit emblazoned with the BLM logo and knelt prior to matches or competitions.[3] The movement gained significant publicity with official endorsements

1

from multinational corporations.[4] The ice-cream maker Ben and Jerry's pledged to 'do all it can to dismantle white supremacy',[5] while elite universities issued statements denouncing their institutional racism. Books like *White Fragility*; *Why I'm No Longer Talking To White People About Race* and *How To Be An Antiracist* became international best sellers. Never has a protest movement generated such interest or had such establishment support.

The extent of this establishment backing is especially surprising given the stated aims of BLM. The UK wing of BLM has a public crowdfunding website that states:

> 'We're guided by a commitment to dismantle imperialism, capitalism, white-supremacy, patriarchy and the state structures that disproportionately harm black people in Britain and around the world. We build deep relationships across the diaspora and strategize to challenge the rise of the authoritarian right-wing across the world, from Brazil to Britain.'[6]

We can only assume that, in 2020, multinational corporations and wealthy individuals alike are relaxed about dismantling capitalism, given the site raised close to £1.25million (as of 25/11/20). BLM campaigns to abolish prisons and defund the police, as well as to remove national borders and raise awareness of climate change.[7] The link between these issues is explained by Ibram X. Kendi, author of *How To Be An Antiracist*:

> 'Do nothing climate policy is racist policy, since predominantly non-White global south is being victimized by climate change more than the Whiter global north is contributing more to its acceleration.'

BLM was founded by three women, Alicia Garza, Patrisse Cullors and Opal Tometi, who met as community organisers and civil rights activists. The phrase 'Black Lives Matter' was first used by Garza in a Facebook post entitled 'A Love Letter to Black People' following the acquittal of George Zimmerman for the killing of Trayvon Martin in 2013.[8] Garza's Facebook post was shared on Twitter by Cullors who tagged it with #BlackLivesMatter. The slogan migrated into a rallying cry for the street protests against police brutality that took place towards the end of 2014 in response to the shootings of Michael Brown and Eric Garner. In 2016, Twitter reported that #BlackLivesMatter was the third most used hashtag related to a social cause in the site's 10-year history.

The Pew Research Center notes that the organisers of BLM 'made social media – and specifically the hashtag #BlackLivesMatter – a centerpiece of their strategy. As a result, the growth of the movement offline was directly linked with the online conversation.'[9] As both a campaigning group and social media hashtag established in response to police brutality against black people, BLM was well positioned to respond to the killing of George Floyd.

Some academics and journalists have questioned the accuracy of claims made by BLM about the relative proportion of black deaths at the hands of police officers. They argue that the portrayal of institutionalised racist brutality within the police force is a 'founding myth' of the BLM movement. Author Wilfred Reilly suggests, 'an almost fact-free narrative of American black "genocide" – to quote prominent attorney Benjamin Crump – is sustained by selective dishonesty and plain old-fashioned censorship on the part of "allies" of the black community.'[10] Likewise, the Manhattan Institute's Heather Mac Donald argues 'there is no epidemic of fatal police shootings against unarmed black Americans.'[11]

Nonetheless, in the summer of 2020, widespread, high profile, institutional support for BLM continued even though many of the protests that took place in the US in the weeks following Floyd's killing were far from peaceful and some descended into riots. Journalist Michael Tracey notes:

'From large metro areas like Chicago and Minneapolis/St. Paul, to small and mid-sized cities like Fort Wayne, Indiana and Green Bay, Wisconsin, the number of boarded up, damaged or destroyed buildings I have personally observed – commercial, civic, and residential – is staggering.'

He continues, 'large swathes of a major American metropolis, Minneapolis/St. Paul, still lie in rubble over a month after the riots.' Yet despite blanket global media coverage of the BLM protests, there was little acknowledgement of any rioting having taken place. In fact, despite visual evidence to the contrary occurring even as they spoke to camera, reporters described the protests as 'peaceful'. Tracey explains, 'media elites desperately do not want to undermine the moral legitimacy of a 'movement' that they have cast as presumptively righteous.'[12]

There are many reasons why BLM has become a lavishly funded, global movement that receives high profile backing and appears largely immune from elite criticism. The name, if not the organisation, is hardly controversial. Few disagree that black lives matter. The official BLM website describes the movement's mission as being, 'to eradicate white supremacy and build local power to intervene in violence inflicted on Black communities by the state and vigilantes.' Again, it is impossible to disagree with such a statement. Phrases such as white supremacy and state-sanctioned violence are designed to garner support. But the moral consensus means questions go unasked. For example, it would be helpful to know: How big a problem is 'white supremacy' and what form does it take nowadays? What form does state violence against black communities take? And who are the vigilantes? Such questions risk appearing pedantic when posed against the widely circulated images of George Floyd's brutal death. But when protesters declare that 'silence is violence' and white supremacy is evident in the school curriculum then it is worth probing the consensus.

The BLM site claims, 'By combating and countering acts of violence, creating space for Black imagination and innovation, and centering Black joy, we are winning immediate improvements in our lives.'[13] These sentences pose a stark contrast between, on the one hand, 'white supremacy,' 'violence' and 'vigilantes' and, on the other, 'imagination,' 'innovation' and 'joy'. White supremacy is assumed as fact, with racism presented as a morally unambiguous conflict between violence and joy. Its rhetoric places BLM within the therapeutic sphere of self-actualisation. Ultimately, the demand is for self-expression; it epitomises a culture of narcissism rather than posing a revolutionary threat to the status quo.

The BLM website claims one of the movement's objectives is to 'fight against elected officials, be they Democrat or Republican, who don't share a vision that is radical and intersectional.' It is critical of previous black liberation movements for having:

> 'created room, space, and leadership mostly for Black heterosexual, cisgender men — leaving women, queer and transgender people, and others, either out of the movement or in the background to move the work forward with little or no recognition.'

Its UK Crowdfunder suggests the group aims are 'to support black life against institutional racism and enable radical reimagining/knowledge production from within our communities.' Again, we see a sharp contrast between the rhetoric of 'fighting against elected officials' on the one hand, and the goal of 'knowledge production' on the other. The radical language masks an individualised and therapeutic pursuit.

References to intersectionality, the division and grouping of people according not just to race but to sexuality and gender identity, to knowledge production and – again – to imagination, firmly position BLM within identity politics and Critical Race Theory (CRT). This would suggest that the BLM movement is more concerned with ideology – and changing how people think – than it is with tackling poverty and material inequalities. From this perspective, white supremacy is located within culture and change comes about through altering perceptions and privileging subjective experience over objective analyses of social problems. Both BLM and CRT have become shorthand for an approach that positions people according to racially ascribed differences, before labelling white people as guilty and black people as victims on account of the privilege/oppression they are said to experience within a system that perpetuates racism.[14]

As such, despite appearing to be radical, BLM aligns with and confirms long-established views on race and racism. As we explore below, far from threatening existing hierarchies, BLM's individualised and therapeutic approach to tackling racism, grounded as it is within CRT, allows elites to gain a renewed sense of moral authority. The mainstreaming and elite-backing of anti-racism initiatives today suggests an understanding of race and racism that resounds with, rather than posing a threat to, existing cultural norms and economic practices. BLM is a relatively new movement and, although CRT has a longer history, it is newly fashionable. Yet the roots of both emerge from assumptions about race relations first found in America in the years following World War Two.

Anti-racism in the past

In the nineteenth and early twentieth century, imperialism, colonial exploitation and slavery were justified by a belief that white people were physically, mentally and morally superior to the people they ruled over. This view, that has since come to be known as 'scientific racism', extended to the working class at home who were portrayed as genetically distinct from and inferior to the upper class. This biological understanding of race began to be called into question after World War Two, although its legacy continued to play out in apartheid South Africa, Jim Crow laws in the American South and discrimination in the UK.

W.E.B. Du Bois, an American sociologist writing in the first decades of the twentieth century, acknowledged the existence of racial differences but argued that it was society in the present, and the historical legacy of differential treatment, that prevented racial equality. He argued that because the American experiment had been largely determined by white founding fathers, black people experienced 'double-consciousness'. In an article in *The Atlantic* he explained that this involved:

'A sense of always looking at one's self through the eyes of others, of measuring one's soul by the tape of a world that looks on in amused contempt and pity. One feels his two-ness, — an American, a Negro; two souls, two thoughts, two unreconciled strivings; two warring ideals in one dark body, whose dogged strength alone keeps it from being torn asunder.'[15]

Du Bois did not seek to eliminate this double-consciousness either by disappearing into or separating off from white

American society. Rather, he argued, the 'American Negro' desires a 'merging':

'He does not wish to Africanize America, for America has too much to teach the world and Africa; he does not wish to bleach his Negro blood in a flood of white Americanism, for he believes—foolishly, perhaps, but fervently—that Negro blood has yet a message for the world. He simply wishes to make it possible for a man to be both a Negro and an American without being cursed and spit upon by his fellows, without losing the opportunity of self-development.'

Through self-development, Du Bois hoped that the black man could become 'a co-worker in the kingdom of culture.'

The desire for black citizens to be 'co-workers' and 'both a Negro and an American' drove the civil rights era challenge to Jim Crow legislation, demands for legal equality and 'colour blind' policies. Colour blindness, rarely understood literally as not 'seeing' racial differences, but rather as not judging people according to race, became a popular idea at this time. It is perhaps best summed up by Martin Luther King Jr. in his famous speech delivered at the Lincoln Memorial, Washington D.C. in August 1963:

'I have a dream that my four little children will one day live in a nation where they will not be judged by the color of their skin but by the content of their character.'[16]

Colour-blindness provided an important challenge to the legal segregation that operated in the US and the overt racism that existed in the UK. In both countries, formal and informal 'colour bars' kept black people out of jobs, housing and schools that were reserved exclusively for white people. Within this context, the demand that people not be judged by the colour of their skin was revolutionary.

Some social change did occur as a result of the demand

for colour blind legal equality but the limits of this approach were soon exposed. For example, after a long battle, in 1954 the US Supreme Court declared racial segregation in public schools to be unconstitutional, meaning that black children could learn alongside white classmates. Derrick Bell, a critical legal scholar and one of the original exponents of CRT, later argued that granting desegregation of schooling, at this point in time, had to do with 'world and domestic considerations – not moral qualms over blacks' plight.'[17] In practice, most schools remained racially divided because of income inequality and segregated housing.

Free speech, democracy and legal equality were initially considered integral to the fight for civil rights. But when the limits of this approach were revealed in the 1960s and into the 1970s, these principles were challenged and new solutions sought. By the end of the 1960s, with both racism and poverty still major problems, groups within the civil rights movement began to question whether legal changes would ever be sufficient to bring about equality. Many arrived at the conclusion that legal equality not only left social inequality intact but provided the context and justification for its continuation. To solve the problem of racial inequality, they had to go further. For some, this meant a greater push for integration and assimilation; they continued to argue for universal human rights and championed initiatives such as 'integration busing'. In 1971, the Supreme Court ruled that States could transport black children to schools in predominantly white neighbourhoods to achieve racially balanced education.

At the same time, a new generation of activists challenged the whole strategy of promoting black assimilation into an existing, white-dominated culture and instead turned to black separatism, or nationalism. As the authors of *Words That Wound* point out:

'It became apparent to many who were active in the civil rights movement that dominant conceptions of race, racism, and equality were increasingly incapable of providing any meaningful quantum of racial justice.'[18]

Only a few years after Martin Luther King Jr. spoke in Washington, the Black Power movement became increasingly influential. Malcolm X, formerly a spokesman for the Nation of Islam, a black nationalist group that emerged in the 1930s, critiqued King's speech and argued instead for a more militant and separatist approach that would not appeal to white people to rescind power, or look for accommodations within existing structures, but would, instead, promote black self-sufficiency and more complete social change.

This marked a significant shift. As Elisabeth Lasch-Quinn points out in *Race Experts*, the waning of the civil rights movement overlapped with the psychotherapy boom, leading to a shift from civil rights universalism to 'the black identity movement'. Black identity was something to be proud of – but in the process of celebration, racial difference was once more made real. Race may no longer have been considered a biological reality, but it rapidly became thought of as an identity created and made real by society. Rather than challenging the basis for the formation of this identity, anti-racists considered it vital to validate and empower the socially constructed self. Race moved from bodies to brains. By the mid-1960s, oppression was considered a state of mind as much as economic exploitation or a denial of equal rights. For some, constructing one's identity became more important than the political project of attaining equality or building community. This change in direction was disastrous for the most positive and forward-looking aims of the civil rights movement, defined by Lasch-Quinn as: 'a democratic nation able to transcend racial and other cleavages; a revived civic culture; and a truly human social order.'

This turn towards identity marked the emergence of another divide within groups challenging racial inequality, between 'realists' who focused upon material inequalities such as housing, schooling, employment and income, and 'idealists' who sought cultural and linguistic change. Although this seems to be a substantive distinction, it increasingly seems that the same conclusions are reached. Both consider words and attitudes to be important in the construction of race and the practice of racism, and both assume that such attitudes have real world consequences, particularly in the allocation of privilege and status. As Delgado and Stefancic make clear, it is assumed that 'racial hierarchies determine who gets tangible benefits, including the best jobs, the best schools, and invitations to parties in people's homes.'[19] This ignores progress made and overlooks other explanations for inequality, for example social class, in preference for assuming people harbour irredeemably racist attitudes. By 1987, Bell argued this point more explicitly: 'progress in American race relations is largely a mirage obscuring the fact that whites continue, consciously or unconsciously, to do all in their power to ensure their dominion and maintain their control.'[20]

The 1980s saw the emergence of a black self-reliance movement. Some black people established their own businesses and, often organising through church or neighbourhood groups, took responsibility for housing, education, medical assistance and welfare provision within their communities. Kendi suggests that this movement was 'a double-edged sword' because it was driven by an assumption that black people were 'entirely capable of ruling themselves' while at the same time representing an assimilationist idea that black communities were at fault and needed to look inwards to their own culture for solutions.[21] Kendi criticises the black civil-rights lawyer Eleanor Homes Norton who, in 1985, wrote in the *New York Times* that the solution to racial inequality was 'not as simple as providing necessities and opportunities' but required the 'overthrow of the complicated, predatory ghetto subculture.' Norton urged not just self-reliance but the positive promotion of values of 'hard work, education, respect for family' and 'achieving a better life for one's children.'[22] Kendi argues, 'The class that challenged racist policies from the 1950s through the 1970s now began challenging other Black people in the 1980s and 1990s.'[23] Today, any discussion of problems within black communities or black culture is taboo.

Kendi traces the promotion of assimilation back to Du Bois and his idea of double consciousness. The process of looking at oneself through the eyes of another racial group, Kendi argues, sets white people up as both 'norm' and judge. Du Bois, Kendi suggests, wanted to liberate black people from racism to change them and save them from their 'relic of barbarism'. All attempts at assimilation are fundamentally racist, Kendi argues, because they position one racial group as superior and insist others aspire to meet its standards.[24] At the same time as the black self-reliance movement was taking off, some activists began to find a home within academia where:

'individual law teachers and students committed to racial justice began to meet, to talk, to write, and to engage in political action in an effort to confront and oppose dominant societal and institutional forces that maintained the structures of racism while professing the goal of dismantling racial discrimination.'[25]

This marked the beginnings of CRT.

The emergence of Critical Race Theory

Critical Race Theory (CRT) is newly fashionable but it has a long and complex history. It began as the pursuit of academics committed to researching and changing attitudes to race and the interplay between racism and power.[26] They merged scholarship from critical legal studies and radical feminism, as well as work by philosophers and theorists associated with Critical Theory more broadly, such as Foucault and Derrida. They combined this with a psychological understanding of race and a therapeutic and behaviouristic approach to race relations that had emerged in the 1960s alongside the civil rights movement.[27]

In their popular primer on CRT, Delgado and Stefancic note that when critical race theory first began to gain traction within academia, 'scholars questioned whether the much-vaunted system of civil rights remedies ended up doing people of color much good.' These academic activists argued that 'majoritarian self-interest' was 'a critical factor in the ebb and flow of civil rights doctrine'; in other words, a white-majority society would be unlikely to cede its power voluntarily.[28] Delgado and Stefancic cite Derrick Bell, Harvard's first African American professor, who argued that 'civil rights advances for blacks always seemed to coincide with changing economic conditions and the self-interest of elite whites,' while more emotional responses to racism, such as 'sympathy' and 'mercy' changed little. A key text to come out of this period was Bell's *Race, Racism and American*

Law, published in 1970. In it, Bell argued white people only concede rights when it is their interests to do so, a notion he labelled 'interest convergence': 'Because racism advances the interests of both white elites (materially) and working-class whites (psychically), large segments of society have little incentive to eradicate it.'[29]

Within academia, black scholars found common cause with professors engaged in critical legal studies who sought to formulate a radical left-wing critique of dominant liberal approaches to the law. Together, they drew from 'liberalism, Marxism, the law and society movement, critical legal studies, feminism, poststructuralism/postmodernism, and neopragmatism.' For some this meant a more idealist turn with a key aim being to examine 'the relationships between naming and reality, knowledge and power.'[30] This marked a distinct turn towards subjectivity and an overlap with work carried out by sensitivity training counsellors who had been promoting therapeutic approaches to race relations in the workplace since the late 1940s. It led to racism being understood not just as legal and economic inequalities, but as social and cultural practices and, above all else, a matter of psychology.

At this point, as Matsuda *et al* tell us:

'Scholars of color within the left began to ask their white colleagues to examine their own racism and to develop oppositional critiques not just to dominant conceptions of race and racism but to the treatment of race within the left as well.'

Their conclusions presented racism:

'not as isolated instances of conscious bigoted decision making or prejudiced practice, but as larger, systemic, structural, and cultural, as deeply psychologically and socially ingrained.'[31]

The foregrounding of the 'vulnerable self' placed a renewed emphasis on the emotional states of both black and white people, how feelings translated into behaviour, and how experts could help individuals better manage their emotions and behaviour to alleviate the consequences of racism across society.

In 1981, Kimberle Crenshaw, then a student of Derrick Bell's, led a protest against Harvard Law School when it refused to hire a black professor to teach *Race, Racism and American Law* following Bell's departure. Crenshaw, along with others, invited leading academics and practitioners of colour to lecture on a course aimed at 'developing a full account of the legal construction of race and racism.' Bringing people together in this joint intellectual project crystalised the ideas underpinning CRT. By the end of the 1980s, Crenshaw's work led her to devise a framework she labelled 'intersectionality' to describe how multiple features of a person's identity can combine to create different modes of discrimination and privilege. Her 1991 essay, *Mapping the margins: intersectionality, identity politics and violence against women of color*, has been highly influential.

Pluckrose and Lindsay point out that the concerns of materialists dominated the critical race movement from the 1970s to the 1980s. However, by the 1990s, a more identity-focused and postmodern understanding of CRT, driven primarily by radical black feminists such as Crenshaw, Audre Lorde, bell hooks, Patricia Hill Collins and Angela Harris, was becoming increasingly popular. Black identity was assumed to be constructed through the collective experience of racism and made manifest through, sometimes deeply repressed, psychological wounds. This re-cast and re-established racial differences at the very point their existence was being challenged most successfully.

Critical Race Theory today

Critical race theorists are not the first to point out that race is socially constructed; that is, it is not a naturally occurring phenomenon but created and made meaningful by people collectively, over time and place. Few today disagree with this point. But whereas a previous generation of anti-racists challenged the significance of biological differences to argue there was one race, the human race, and emphasised universal traits that create a common humanity irrespective of skin colour, critical race theorists argue that once constructed, race becomes an uncontestable fact. As Robin Di Angelo, author of *White Fragility*, explains, 'While there is no biological race as we understand it, race as a social construct has profound significance and shapes every aspect of our lives.'[32] According to Ibram X. Kendi, race is 'a power construct of blended difference that lives socially.' He explains:

> 'I still identify as Black. Not because I believe Blackness, or race, is a meaningful scientific category but because our societies, our policies, our ideas, our histories, and our cultures have rendered race and made it matter.'[33]

This raises the question of who, or what processes, are responsible for constructing race. Kendi argues, 'Race creates new forms of power: the power to categorize and judge, elevate and downgrade, include and exclude. Race makers use that power to process distinct individuals, ethnicities, and nationalities into monolithic races.'[34] Once, 'race makers' were the white social and political elite who sought to justify slavery or colonialism. But who are the race makers today?

Di Angelo and Kendi promote an inescapably circular argument whereby race is constructed and made meaningful through racism; it is people's everyday experiences within a racist society that create the reality of race. According to law professor Kendall Thomas:

> 'We are raced. We are acted upon and constructed by racist speech. The meaning of Black or white is derived through a history of acted upon ideology.'[35]

When race is socially constructed through racist attitudes, racism is understood as systemic; that is, built into the very fabric of societies designed by white people, for the benefit of white people. Proponents of CRT argue that ideas of white superiority and black inferiority are intrinsic to our language, culture and interpretations of history. In this way, racial differences come to be entrenched and individuals become subsumed into a racialised group identity.

According to this teaching, ideas of individual autonomy, resilience and effort are 'a racist myth'[36] and rather than people's lives being determined by their own will, they are determined by factors beyond their control: white privilege and black oppression. This traps everyone in what Lasch-Quinn refers to as 'the harangue-flagellation ritual' in which black people are put 'in the role of repressed, angry victims' and white people 'in the role of oppressors who need to expiate their guilt.' Whereas the earlier incarnation of the civil rights movement held out the prospect of overcoming racial differences, the psychologising of race ensures racial differences are never eradicated. The best we can strive for is healing and acceptance, performed through the correct etiquette and mediated by a burgeoning army of race experts.

Today, CRT has migrated from academia and into the mainstream alongside the rise of both identity politics and a more therapeutic cultural ethos. As such, terms like 'structural racism' now refer to structures of thought far more than any structural, material analysis of society. Experts have taken the subjective, identitarian and psychological understanding of racism developed within universities and transformed it into a list of commandments all must obey.

Critical race theorists may not see race as a biological fact but they do view it as an ingrained outlook, endemic in culture and imprinted on the consciousness of every individual. Consequently, they do not consider that racism will be reduced by challenging individual instances of prejudice; instead, the entire social hierarchy must be overturned. As Delgado and Stefancic suggest, this marks a sharp break from the traditional civil rights discourse, 'which stresses incrementalism and step-by-step progress'; instead:

> 'critical race theory questions the very foundations of the liberal order, including equality theory, legal reasoning, Enlightenment rationalism, and neutral principles of constitutional law.'[37]

CRT stands in opposition to values of objectivity, neutrality, equality and meritocracy. Personal, or 'lived' experience is privileged over objectivity because it is assumed that people cannot understand the world other than from the standpoint of their identity group. Revisionist history is employed to bring to the fore past psychological wounds that are assumed still to reverberate today and to promote a positive identity in the present.

Revisionist History

One of CRT's founding assumptions is that 'whiteness', the values and beliefs that arise from the lived experiences of being white in a white-majority society, needs to be continually challenged. The normalisation of whiteness means experts are required to identify problematic attitudes and to lead people towards greater racial sensitivity and correct ways of thinking and behaving towards one another. Education is seen as a useful starting point with a particular focus upon how history can be used to re-write national narratives of racial identity. Delgado and Stefancic make a case for 'revisionist history' which, they argue 'reexamines America's historical record, replacing comforting majoritarian interpretations of events with ones that square more accurately with minorities' experiences.'

One task of the revisionist historian is to 'unearth little-known chapters of racial struggle, sometimes in ways that reinforce current reform efforts.'[38] One of the most well-known revisionist histories, designed for use in the school curriculum, is the *New York Times'* '1619 project'.

The 1619 project involved re-writing history to position 1619, the arrival of the first slave ships in Virginia, and not 1776 and the Declaration of Independence, as the founding of America. This change is significant because it suggests that the entire 'American experiment' is not founded on the ideas set out in the Declaration, such as that 'all men are created equal' but on a far more damning concept of white supremacy and black enslavement. Its lead researcher, Nikole Hannah-Jones, argues that every important event in American history, up to and including the Civil War, was designed to protect or advance slavery.[39] Several scholars have pointed out the numerous inaccuracies in the 1619 project, most notably Peter Wood, who argues that the proper starting point for the American story is 1620, with the signing of the Mayflower Compact aboard ship before the Pilgrims set foot in the Massachusetts wilderness.[40] However, the influential and well-funded 1619 project continues to be taught in schools across the US.

In the UK, there are repeated calls, stretching back over decades, to make the school curriculum more diverse. Significant steps have been taken in this direction but the teaching of history continues to be a particular focus for campaigners with, most recently, calls for History GCSE to be given a 'Black Lives Matter makeover'.[41] At all levels of education but especially in universities, activists cohere around the demand to 'decolonise the curriculum'.

Campaigners argue that universities must acknowledge and take steps to ameliorate the 'structural and epistemological legacy' of colonialism. The decolonise movement, which rapidly spread off campus, focuses on the removal of statues and plaques commemorating historical figures who rose to fame and fortune through the brutal exploitation of the colonies. The *Rhodes Must Fall* campaign has called for statues of the imperialist Cecil Rhodes to be torn down from the University of Oxford in the UK and the University of Cape Town in South Africa. Individual universities in the UK, such as SOAS and Sussex, have their own decolonise campaigns, and in the USA there have been campaigns to have buildings and institutions founded from the financial legacy of the slave trade renamed.

Beyond this, the decolonisation movement seeks to interrogate the very nature of knowledge propagated through higher education.[42] The content of the curriculum, campaigners argue, continues to reflect and perpetuate a colonial legacy, through the presentation of a white, western intellectual tradition as not just superior to other forms of knowledge but as universal. Movements to decolonise teaching, such as 'Why is my curriculum white?' which began at University College London, draw attention to the prevalence of white males especially on humanities programmes such as philosophy. The privileging of Kant,

Plato and Descartes, they suggest, normalises a Euro-centric and Enlightenment-focused view of the world.[43] This presents colonialism not as an episode from history, but as a real impingement upon the present. The organisers of *Rhodes Must Fall at Oxford*, argue: 'A lot of the time when people talk about colonialism they think of it as a past event that happened. They don't think about it as something that manifests itself in everyday life at institutions like Oxford.'[44] This appears to pitch politically radical students against irredeemably racist institutions full of pale, male and stale academics. In practice, however, students often find their views on curricular matters are solicited at every turn by academics at the forefront of championing decolonisation.[45] Many are all too ready to jettison traditional curricular. The pervasive influence of Critical Theory within humanities departments means that works of literature and philosophy are often perceived as simply 'texts' to be dissected rather than ideas to be imbibed. In this regard, rather than posing a challenge to institutions, the decolonise the curriculum movement is simply confirming mainstream academic thought. Both academics and students share the same intention: to decentralise the western intellectual tradition in favour of teaching content that can be shown to represent biological, rather than intellectual, diversity.

The enthusiasm with which this project has been grasped represents academics' embarrassment at attempts to preserve and pass on intellectual traditions, that, though they may have emanated in the west, were once considered to be of universal value. It represents a loss of faith in their ability to differentiate some knowledge as superior. Instead, we have an apparent relativism that appears, on the surface, to present the works of different thinkers or different schools of thought as being of equal worth.

However, in the eyes of decolonisers, not all knowledge is of equal value. Truth is no longer determined by objective measures but is a matter of 'lived experience'. In this way, identity determines what deserves to be known. Decolonise academia movements insist epistemological judgements should be based on identity rather than objective measures of truth or intellectual merit. Instead of looking at what Hegel or Du Bois, Audre Lorde or Sylvia Plath, have to offer in terms of their contribution to knowledge, we are asked to make crude judgements based on sex and skin colour with white and male being bad, black and female being better.

The closer knowledge is to truth and the more it is considered to be universally relevant, the more worthy it should be of a place in the curriculum. To argue that 'universal truth' is a myth and that truth is identity-dependent is to give up on the goals of education entirely – it is to suggest we have nothing to learn from previous generations or from each other. We can only indulge in the narcissistic enterprise of exploring our individual truths within our personal context. There are many good reasons to review and change what goes on in universities. The decolonise higher education movement is not among them. It represents a retrogressive view of knowledge; it entrenches racial thinking and presents a degraded view of black students. It prompts a censoriousness driven by the demand that statues and curricular content be removed to white-wash the past in favour of a re-racialised present.[46]

Lived experience

Critical race theorists consider 'lived experience' to be the most significant factor in ascertaining the nature and extent of racism. It is the social meaning ascribed to groups that is said to create differences in people's lived experiences;

in other words, as a woman I will experience the world differently to men because men and women are treated differently in society. In relation to race, it is because black people are treated differently to white people that they, in turn, come to experience the world differently. Having first been constructed, and then made public, lived experience carries the status of truth. As Delgado and Stefancic explain, 'because of their different histories and experiences with oppression, black, American Indian, Asian, and Latino writers and thinkers may be able to communicate to their white counterparts matters that the whites are unlikely to know. Minority status, in other words, brings with it a presumed competence to speak about race and racism.'[47]

'Lived experience' is another term that has migrated from academia into everyday life. It is used as a methodological approach to qualitative research in disciplines such as sociology; although there are disputes over how best to capture and record participants' lived experiences. However, it is increasingly used as an everyday position statement by activists to refer to bringing their own perceptions, understandings and experiences to bear on a situation. For example, upon being elected Vice President of the US in November 2020, Kamala Harris told a TV interviewer that she had promised Joe Biden to always share with him her 'lived experience, as it relates to any issue that we confront'.[48] As the philosopher Kwame Anthony Appiah points out, when the phrase 'lived experience' first crossed from academia to activism, it was used almost exclusively 'to designate firsthand experiences that were specific to women, minorities and other vulnerable groups.' However, it is now used far more liberally to describe anyone's perspective while still assuming power in 'the unappealable authority' it represents. As Appiah notes:

'You can debate my sociopolitical analyses – those facts and interpretations are shared and public – but not my lived experience. Lived experience isn't something you argue, it's something you have.'[49]

As lived experience is only known to the individual concerned, it is an incontestable truth and, as such, is more true than mere attempts at objective measurement. There are several problems with this approach to academic research, policy, and activism. Experience 'is never unmediated and self-interpreting'; we interpret and re-present our experiences according to our beliefs and prior understandings. Furthermore, no one person's experiences can truly be representative of general phenomenon. We meet the world as individuals. Even though we may share age, sex, class, sexuality or other features of our identity with others, we are no more a product of these features than we are a product of our biology. The assumption that there is a common female, black, or queer experience risks falling back upon stereotypes.[50] The author David Goodhart describes lived experience as a type of knowledge but one that is 'highly constrained and even misleading'. It is the unreliability of personal testimony (anecdote) that makes facts, data, and objective knowledge so important in understanding the world. As Goodhart points out, 'We may then select the data based on our own interests or worldview — indeed it is almost impossible not to — but at least we are making some effort to use the apparatus of objectivity: logic and evidence.'[51]

According to critical race theorists, lived experience is a more valid form of truth than objective knowledge and therefore a superior way of gaining insight into the nature of racism. However, the lack of objectivity makes it difficult to assess the extent of racism and therefore to make comparisons over time. This does not mean that critical race theorists avoid all use of data. Rather, data becomes a supplement to, and occasionally a measure of, lived experience. Kendi tells us:

'White people are more likely than Black and Latinx people to sell drugs, and the races consume drugs at similar rates. Yet African Americans are far more likely than Whites to be jailed for drug offenses.'[52]

But this raises several questions: Are African Americans more likely to be jailed as a proportion of the population, or as a proportion of those convicted? Are black and white people equally as likely to plead guilty? Or to have equivalent legal advice? Such statistics highlight racial disparities without necessarily proving racism to be their cause.

For critical race theorists, lived experience also constitutes the basis for racism. White people are said to have a shared lived experience that determines how they make sense of the world and is different from the lived experience of black people. Racially distinct experiences produce racially distinct understandings. As our actions are said to be determined by our knowledge and understanding, then prejudice, even unconscious prejudice, is assumed always to show up in our behaviour. This paves the way for an understanding of racism that can sometimes only be perceived by black people. As Binna Kandola explains in *Racism at Work*:

'Racism has not been eradicated, despite the enormous strides taken over the past fifty years. It has mutated into new and subtler forms and has found new ways to survive. The racism in organisations today is not characterised by hostile abuse and threatening behaviour. It is not overt nor is it obvious. Today, racism is subtle and nuanced, detected mostly by the people on the receiving end, but ignored and possibly not even seen by perpetrators and bystanders.'[53]

When racism is reduced to microaggressions (for example, shifts in tone of voice, misplaced compliments or questions perceived to be inappropriate) it can only be detected by those who are sensitive to its presence, either through their lived experience of racism or after having undertaken training in CRT.

Emphasising the different lived experiences of black and white people, with only one group having true insight into racism, confirms the rejection of 'colour blindness'. 'Colour-blindess' is now criticised for only ever challenging the most blatant forms of discrimination.[54] Kendi argues:

> 'The common idea of claiming 'color blindness' is akin to the notion of being 'not racist' – as with the 'not racist' the color blind individual, by ostensibly failing to see race, fails to see racism and falls into racist passivity. The language of 'color blindness' – like the language of 'not racist' – is a mask to hide racism.'[55]

This stark accusation, that not seeing race is an example of racism and an illustration of white privilege, has become a key argument in the popular understanding of CRT.

White privilege/fragility

CRT demands that, having rejected colour-blindness, people must first and foremost see themselves and others as racialised beings within a system that constructs white people as privileged and black people as oppressed. Di Angelo explains that: 'we live in a society that is deeply separate and unequal by race, and white people are the beneficiaries of that separation and inequality' because they are 'socialized into a deeply internalized sense of superiority.' This view of society-wide racial inequality means that even though individual white people may be against racism, they are still perceived to benefit from a system that privileges whites as a group.

Renni Eddo-Lodge, author of *Why I'm No Longer Talking to White People About Race*, explains: 'if you're white, your race will almost certainly positively impact your life's trajectory in some way. And you probably won't even notice it.'[56] This is because, according to the critical race theorists, whiteness is primarily a standpoint, that is, a set of cultural practices that benefit white people by positioning them as the norm, with black people as a deviation from this norm. In this way, as Di Angelo puts it, 'Whiteness has psychological advantages that translate into material returns.' For white children, the process of socialisation into a 'deeply internalized sense of superiority' is said to begin from the earliest days of infancy. As Di Angelo makes clear: 'I have a white frame of reference and a white world view, and I move through the world with a white experience.'[57] It is this very 'ordinariness' of the white lived experience that makes it so problematic in the minds of critical race theorists.

Proponents of CRT argue that the rhetoric of objectivity and meritocracy allows white people to deny the privileges they are afforded because of their skin colour. When confronted with their privilege, and their apparent deep-rooted sense of superiority and its associated material returns are challenged, white people demonstrate 'fragility'. White fragility is conceptualised as 'a response or 'condition' produced and reproduced by the continual social and material advantages of whiteness.'[58] The focus on whiteness indicates another shift prompted by the reification of the psychology of race: 'whiteness', and not simply racism, is now the problem and as an immutable characteristic, it is irresolvable and requires permanent acts of contrition. As Di Angelo puts it: 'a positive white identity is an impossible goal. White identity is inherently racist; white people do not exist outside the system of white supremacy.'[59]

When racism is viewed in this way, it cannot be challenged through individual white people not being racist; instead, white people must be actively anti-racist. Anti-racism starts with white people acknowledging their own racism and battling the fragility prompted by threats to their privilege. From here, white people must probe deep into their psyches to root out unconscious bias before finally, in seeking to build the world anew, thinking carefully about the new reality constructed with each word uttered. Critical race theorists have reinvented racism. Only this time around, it is not black people that are considered a problem, but white people.

2.

The Anti-Racism Industry

Today, CRT provides a burgeoning group of diversity trainers, race experts and assorted professional anti-racists with the ideas that substantiate their practice within schools, universities and the workplace. The foundational premise of this anti-racism industry is that race is real and racism is endemic. It is, they claim, evident in the disparities that can be noted between comparable performance of different ethnic groups when it comes to school success, career progression, salary and a host of other measurable outcomes. This modern-day clerisy holds that every aspect of our daily lives, from education, policing, the health service and employment, assumes 'whiteness' as the norm, thereby rendering liberal notions of equality meaningless. As a result, they suggest, differences between groups that cannot be otherwise accounted for must be a product of racism and it is the duty of the government to legislate such inequalities out of existence.[60] This may require enforcing new forms of discrimination or race separatism. As Conservative Equalities Minister Kemi Badenoch argues, 'some of the authors and proponents of critical race theory – actually want a segregated society.'[61]

Despite – or perhaps because of – this divisiveness, the 'anti-racism training industry' is proving to be highly lucrative: its high profile 'successful entrepreneurs', people such as DiAngelo and Kendi in the US, Eddo-Lodge and Afua Hirsch in the UK, earn vast sums of money through books and workshops.[62] One report claims that DiAngelo 'has likely made over $2 million from her book,' but that 'the speaking circuit is where she is cleaning up. ... a 60-90 minute keynote would run to $30,000, a two-hour workshop $35,000, and a half-day event $40,000.' It goes on to note: 'Ibram X. Kendi, whose book has jockeyed with DiAngelo's on the bestseller list, charges $150 for tickets to public events and $25,000 for a one-hour presentation ... Former *Atlantic* writer Ta-Nehisi Coates has charged between $30,000 and $40,000 for public lectures.'[63]

Below these race entrepreneurs come the academics, experts and workplace trainers that comprise the burgeoning anti-racism industry. These are professionals who run diversity training programmes in the workplace, universities or schools, or on behalf of voluntary organisations and charities. Some may be 'in house', that is, they are employed as part of the human resources team of a large company or organisation and run anti-racism training sessions alongside other workshops such as health and safety or first aid in the workplace. Other race experts, to employ Lasch-Quinn's term, may be employed by organisations specifically established to provide diversity training and may go out to schools, universities and workplaces, or may host attendees in central venues, or may deliver online content for people to access remotely. The *Harvard Business Review* notes that today, 'Virtually all Fortune 500 companies offer diversity training to their employees.'[64] One study suggests that over 80 per cent of all companies now offer staff unconscious bias training.[65]

The many thousands of people employed in the global diversity industry may not be millionaires but they make a good living and find an important sense of purpose in revealing our unconscious bias, hearing penance and holding out the promise of absolution. There is no formal route to becoming a race expert and no one organisation offering accreditation. Race experts come from a range of academic and professional backgrounds. The most important qualification appears to be lived experience of racism, however far back in the expert's personal biography or however seemingly slight. The imperative of personal experience does not, of course, bar white people from becoming race experts. They must simply specialise in 'the psychosis of whiteness'.[66]

Despite the huge growth in the number of race experts and the near ubiquity of diversity training across public sector and private corporations, there is little evidence that anti-racism training has a positive impact in the workplace. The *Harvard Business Review* notes that of all the Fortune 500 companies offering diversity training, 'surprisingly few of them have measured its impact.' It continues, 'That's unfortunate, considering evidence has shown that diversity training can backfire, eliciting defensiveness from the very people who might benefit most. And even when the training is beneficial, the effects may not last after the program ends.'[67] A review commissioned by the Government Equalities Office in 2020 to analyse the effectiveness of unconscious bias training found that 'there is currently no evidence that this training changes behaviour in the long term or improves workplace equality in terms of representation of women, ethnic minorities or other minority groups.' Worse, it concluded, such training sometimes had unintended 'negative consequences'. In December 2020, the civil service scrapped unconscious bias training (UBT) and urged other public sector employers to do the same.[68]

One reason not to measure the impact of diversity training is that race experts have become so morally and financially invested in the existence of racism, they cannot afford for it ever to disappear. It is perhaps with this in mind that Kendi makes clear, 'Being an anti-racist requires persistent self-awareness, constant self-criticism, and regular self-examination.'[69] CRT lends academic legitimacy to the race experts and provides a theoretical basis for the content of their literature and workshops. Their practice, on the other hand, draws from techniques that originate within therapy and counselling. Lasch-Quinn argues that from the emergence of sensitivity training in the 1940s, through to encounter groups in the 1960s, the ritualised practices that now epitomise the diversity industry, 'cannot be understood apart from the culture of therapy'.[70] She suggests that, in the 1960s, 'psychotherapeutic techniques became widely accepted as appropriate for an ever broadening range of everyday issues or "life problems,"' based on ideas that had been developed in the decades beforehand. Race relations comprised one such 'life problem' considered resolvable through therapeutic practices and mediated by experts who offered enlightenment through training.

The therapeutic practice that forms the basis for most diversity training means familiar patterns are observed irrespective of the specific title or topic of the workshop. To introduce new ways of thinking and behaving towards others, people must first be made self-conscious about their existing relationships. People are taught to see themselves not as individuals, nor as friends and colleagues with interests in common, but as representatives of racial groups. Then, with spontaneity replaced by self-consciousness, attention is drawn to the differences between groups. Sometimes this process involves participants being asked to verbalise stereotypes they have encountered – even if they do not, nor ever have, accepted or reinforced those stereotypes themselves. What comes next is neither critical analysis nor any attempt to challenge or interrogate the stereotypes expressed. Instead, participants are informed that there are racialised differences in the emotional responses people demonstrate when confronted with such stereotypes: black anger and white guilt.

Trainers then lead participants through a process of acceptance and validation of these emotional responses. Lasch-Quinn argues that black anger and white guilt are validated on the assumption that no individual is responsible for their feelings: it is society that has created stereotypes and fuels prejudice. When it is accepted that stereotypes, not individuals, are responsible for racism then the trainer can offer instruction in approved interracial etiquette that focuses upon acknowledging and managing emotional responses in an acceptable way.

The primary criticism made of the diversity training industry is that it simply does not work. It does not improve race relations and it does not lead to greater racial equality. Worse than this, and as explored below, diversity training may increase discrimination. According to one report: 'Firms with diversity training end up with fewer minorities in management, and field research finds that training both reinforces stereotypes and increases animosity against minority groups.'[71] However, expecting diversity training to reduce instances of racism may be to miss the point. Entrenching what Lasch-Quinn refers to as the 'harangue/ flagellation ritual' requires not a solution to racism but a reconciliation to its existence and a commitment to seeking it out where it remains hidden, thereby exposing yet more problems to be resolved through further rounds of training.

Any criticism of this process is put down to 'white fragility' and serves as evidence of the need for yet more training. The sole aim of the diversity industry thus appears to be its own self-perpetuation. Each new iteration provides additional moral weight and, of course, revenue, for the professional anti-racists.

As will be shown below, the diversity industry is now embedded within schools, universities and the workplace. Its reach extends to many millions of citizens across the globe. Online diversity training programmes target many more. Generic diversity training gives way to more specific varieties focusing on implicit or unconscious bias, microaggressions, allyship and active bystander training. Here we consider the nature and content of different forms of training and consider the experiences of participants in particular programmes.

Schools

Evidence of racism in schools falls into three main categories: an ethnicity attainment gap, the over-representation of BAME pupils in school exclusions, and microaggressions located within seemingly neutral curriculum, uniform and behaviour policies. As will be explored below, that racism is the cause of ethnic disparities is often accepted as an article of faith. The *Runnymede Trust's School Report* explains that:

'Concerns over structural racism, low educational attainment, poor teacher expectations and stereotyping, ethnocentric curricula and high levels of school exclusions for some groups remain entrenched features of our school system.'[72]

It is often assumed that BAME pupils struggle within a structurally racist education system with a 'white' curriculum and therefore underperform academically in comparison to their white classmates. However, the data on academic attainment reveals a far more complex and nuanced picture. When it comes to school success, BAME pupils are not one homogenous group. Chinese, Bangladeshi and Indian pupils perform better at GCSE level than white British pupils.[73] We cannot even generalise about all black students. As Richard Norrie notes in *How We Think About Disparity*:

'black Caribbean children do worse than white British ones in school, in terms of attainment. But black Africans do as well, if not marginally better. In 2017/18, 26.9 per cent of black Caribbean pupils achieved a 'strong pass' in GCSE maths and English, compared to 42.7 per cent of white British and 44.3 per cent of black African pupils.'

Such statistics show that while ethnic disparities certainly do exist, it is far from clear that they can be explained simply by racism. Norrie argues:

'the idea that disparity is explained by the curriculum being culturally inappropriate due to its Eurocentrism, or is somehow 'colonial', does not bear up since many ethnic minority groups out-perform the white British.'[74]

Even the Runnymede Trust acknowledges: 'Children from ethnic minorities do well in school in general. This is not to deny that some ethnic minority groups do less well, pupils with Black Caribbean heritage for example.'[75]

School exclusions, either temporary, fixed-term suspensions, or permanent exclusions, are also considered evidence of systemic racism within the education system. Again, we must be careful not to treat all BAME pupils as one homogenous group. The *Timpson Review of School Exclusion* notes:

'some ethnic groups are associated with a lower likelihood of being permanently excluded, including Bangladeshi and

Indian children who are around half as likely to be excluded as White British children. Children from other ethnic groups are more likely to experience exclusion, in particular Black Caribbean and Mixed White and Black Caribbean pupils. … black Caribbean children are 3 times more likely to be expelled than white British children.'[76]

Statistics can highlight ethnic disparities but tell us little about their cause. It cannot tell us whether black Caribbean pupils are more likely to be excluded for demonstrating the same behaviour as their white classmates or whether black Caribbean pupils are more likely to fall foul of school rules. If black Caribbean pupils are more likely to be in breach of behaviour codes, we do not know whether this is because of social and cultural attitudes to school and authority or whether the specific rules being imposed are inherently discriminatory.

Despite this confusion, *The Timpson Review* makes two recommendations in order to tackle ethnic disparities in school exclusions: an increase in the ethnic diversity of school leadership and the creation of 'inclusive environments' for children coming from groups for which exclusion is a particular problem. As Norrie points out: 'The argument is greater diversity and inclusion will cause these children to behave themselves better.' But, he continues,

'there are groups – black African, Pakistani, Bangladeshi, Indian – for whom schools are no more diverse or inclusive and for whom expulsion is extremely rare. It is clear that a lack of 'diversity and inclusion' does not cause bad behaviour, so there is no reason to believe that more of it will cause good behaviour.'[77]

Rather than asking potentially troubling questions about differing cultural attitudes towards education and authority, it is far easier for anti-racism campaigners to argue that schools are places of 'entrenched racial stereotyping and discrimination'.[78]

Educationalists and campaigners alike have been concerned about racial disparities in educational outcomes for several decades. Issues of representation in the curriculum, reading lists, school displays and the identity of staff have all been considered at length. We might reasonably expect that if straightforward solutions were possible, they would have been found and implemented by now. Increasingly, CRT provides a theoretical and ideological focus for staff and pupil workshops to run alongside existing diversity and inclusion initiatives.

In June 2020, Channel 4 screened *The School That Tried to End Racism*, a documentary series that followed the progress of children made to undergo anti-racist training based upon principles of CRT.[79] This was the first UK trial of a US programme aimed at educating pupils in unconscious racial bias. It took place at a nonselective state secondary school in London with a diverse pupil intake. The children were filmed completing tasks such as attaching negative and positive words to pictures of faces from different ethnic groups and dividing into 'affinity groups' (white students in one, black and brown students in another) to discuss what racial identity means. One task the children are set involves them taking up starting positions in a race according to their answers to certain questions. They are told, for example, to 'Take a step forward if you've never been asked where you come from.' 'Step back if you have ever worried about stop and search'. 'Step forward if you've never been the only person your colour in a room'. This exercise is intended to introduce children to the concept of white privilege.

It becomes obvious from early in the programme that

many of the children have never considered themselves as members of racial groups before being told to organise in this way. Indeed, for quite a few of the children this is no easy matter: those of mixed heritage are uncertain which group they are expected to join. The message, driven home with ever increasing explicitness, is that black and brown people are inherently disdavantaged and white people inherently privileged. The participants are forced to relate these categories to themselves; despite still being children they are either disadvantaged, a victim of social forces, or privileged. The dawning realisation of guilt/victimhood is played out on camera for the gratification of viewers.

This series raises ethical implications that go far beyond a child's ability to consent to participating in what is, essentially, a reality television show. There are significant ethical questions to be asked about subjecting children to this form of anti-racism training. We can assume their participation was either mandatory or became effectively mandatory through pressure to conform. The consequences of racialising children, having them recite stereotypes, before inculcating victimhood/guilt based on biological characteristics they have no control over, are either not considered or assumed to be beneficial. The US academic John McWhorter asks:

'Why would anyone voluntarily send their children to be taught that they are guilty regardless of their decency and kindness? A school where they are constantly reminded of the color of their skin, not the content of their character. What Black parent wants the other children to feel sorry for their kid and look at them differently?'[80]

Mark is a secondary school teacher:
'The school I was working in a couple of years ago ran staff training on equity. The area the school is based in is not at all racially diverse and so quite a lot of the focus was on social class. We did a few exercises like a privilege walk, we had to take steps forward and backward in answer to questions like how many wage earners there were in our household, whether we were a refugee or an immigrant. This was organised by our local education authority and it was building on themes they had been running with for a number of years. The good thing is that no one really felt singled out by this.

'Sometimes it seems like these initiatives are put in place simply for the sake of being seen to do something and as if some of these ideas just get made up by whoever is organising the session. Most teachers are not at all political, they are not really activists. They are just nice people who want to get on with the job and they don't have any natural inclination to question all the latest buzzwords. On top of this, many teachers just don't really know all that much about history or politics and so they can end up making well-intentioned mistakes.

'I expect things would have been very different if this same training had been carried out this summer, there has been much more concern about race and racism in schools this year, especially since Black Lives Matter took off in the summer.

'We have had FGM awareness training which I think is mandatory every couple of years and we have also had Prevent training. They both tend to take a very general approach and broaden out to cover all kinds of political or religious views without really focusing on any one religion or viewpoint in particular. Some teaching unions are pushing for us all to have diversity training and unconscious bias training and they are encouraging us to talk about systemic racism and issues like that.'

Although, as this report illustrates, there are questions to be asked of anti-racism training based on principles of CRT in any setting, there are specific concerns to be addressed when this form of training is used in schools. Establishing a white guilt/black victimhood framework in children who are not yet responsible for their own actions and have not yet had opportunity to make an impact on the world can be damaging. Government Equalities Minister Kemi Badenoch has argued, 'The repetition of the victimhood narrative is really poisonous for young people because they hear it and believe it.'[81] For black children, learning that they are at a disadvantage, and that a racist 'system' is stacked against them, may mean they are less inclined to try to begin with.

Universities

Racism in universities is said to be evidenced by the under-representation of BAME students either across the higher education sector as a whole or within certain institutions or disciplines; as well as by the under-representation of black academics, particularly at senior levels. Other areas of concern include the ethnicity attainment gap, the 'white' curriculum and the prevalence of racist microaggressions. Anti-racist training in higher education primarily aims to encourage academics to prioritise representation and diversity, particularly in relation to decolonising the curriculum, and alter teaching and assessment practice away from what is assumed to be a 'white norm'. There is also an emphasis on tackling unconscious bias and microaggressions from staff, students and at the level of the institution.

There are several problems with this approach. First, some of the assumptions that are made do not stand up to scrutiny. Advance HE is a charity that promotes equality in higher education through the accreditation of teaching and learning programmes, Athena SWAN, and the Race Equality Charter. Their research into the ethnicity attainment gap suggests that white British students are more likely to receive the highest degree classifications than UK-domiciled students from minority ethnic groups: 'In 2015/16, the gap was largest in England, where 78.8% of white qualifiers received a first/2:1 compared with 63.2% of BME qualifiers – a 15.6 percentage point gap.' However, they go on to acknowledge:

> 'outcomes vary considerably by ethnic group, with particularly wide gaps observed between white and black students in relation to degree attainment. In 2015/16, data shows that:
> - 72.2% of Chinese students were awarded a top degree (a degree attainment gap of 6.6 percentage points)
> - 70.7% of Indian students (a gap of 8.1 percentage points)
> - 61.8% of Pakistani students (a gap of 17.0 percentage points)
> - 50.5% of Black Other students (a gap of 28.3 percentage points)'[82]

In a 2020 report for *Civitas*, academic Ruth Mieschbuehler argues that:

> 'what appears to be a significant gap when attainment is reported by ethnicity has been shown to be significantly reduced when other factors known to impact on attainment are taken into account. There is no statistical evidence that 'ethnicity' determines educational attainment of higher education students.'

Factors that might impact upon final degree classification include: prior attainment including nature of qualification; subject choice; choice of institution; parental support and term time employment. The more such factors are accounted for, the smaller ethnicity alone appears to be a factor in determining attainment.

The problem Mieschbuehler highlights is that the more 'policymakers and practitioners believe in the ethnic attainment gap,' the more likely they are to introduce measures to address it – often with adverse consequences. The danger is that students come to be defined by their skin colour and grouped according to ethnicity. The result is that campus relations become increasingly racialised, which 'drives a wedge between people and removes any sense of our common humanity.' Perhaps even worse for ethnic minority students, this 'new type of 'deficit talk' depicts students as being vulnerable – and ultimately, it denies students the opportunity to develop fully academically while accommodating them to failure.'[83]

Despite the potential problems with such research, new reports purporting to demonstrate the widespread problem with racism in higher education appear frequently. According to a 2020 report from Universities UK, an umbrella group representing all of the UK's universities:

'almost a quarter of students from minority ethnic backgrounds reported experiencing racial harassment. Over half of staff who had experienced racial harassment described incidents of being ignored or excluded because of their race, and nearly a third had experienced racist name-calling, insults and jokes. Both staff and students reported regular experience of microaggressions (ie, subtle, less 'overt' forms of racism). Racial harassment occurred in a wide variety of settings and from multiple harassers.'[84]

Writing in *The Guardian* in 2019, Professor of Black Studies Kehinde Andrews points to a separate report and claims:

'Racial harassment, from open abuse to more passive mistreatment, is so commonplace in UK universities that for black staff members such as myself, it feels like something we just have to get used to. With the publication of the Equality and Human Rights Commission's new report, we now have evidence to prove that racism is grossly under-acknowledged in universities. The figures show that, somehow, 43% and 56% of universities thought that every incident of racial harassment against students and staff was reported. In reality less than half of staff said they had reported their experiences.'[85]

It seems that despite all the decolonise campaigns, awareness raising and diversity champions instigated in recent years, UK universities still 'perpetuate institutional racism' and provide fertile ground for racial harassment which severely impacts the mental health, educational outcomes and career progression of black staff and students. Such assumptions – and conclusions – only begin to make sense when we learn from the UUK report that:

'This guidance draws on the framework of critical race theory. This proposes that racism is an ordinary rather than abnormal experience, supported by societal structures, and that concepts such as 'colour blindness' will only rectify the most overt forms of racism while maintaining structural inequalities. In addition, white people, who as a collective group benefit from structural racism overall, can be complicit (albeit unwittingly) in perpetuating racism and thereby have a responsibility to counter it.'

In other words, racism – primarily in the form of microaggressions – is 'normal', endemic and subjectively experienced – yet it is also a threat to the safety of black staff and students. UUK present 'lived experience' as uncontestable truth. This means that if an incident is perceived as racist then it is treated as such, irrespective of intention. Racism on campus is ubiquitous and yet can often only be detected by those with certain lived experiences or who have undergone specific training to detect its presence.

UUK's *Tackling Racial Harassment in Higher Education* seeks 'to address racial harassment and make our universities safe places to work and study.' When racism is, thankfully, rare, it must be found. UUK recommend that vice-chancellors, academics and all members of staff should undergo diversity and anti-racism training. This training is to encapsulate 'concepts of white privilege, fragility and allyship, and intersectionality.' As part of this training, black students are to be taught to see themselves as victims of racism. They must be taught that if a white friend expresses surprise to see you are both taking the same module; or asks where you are from; or congratulates you for doing well on a test; or says they like your hair, then you are a victim of racial harassment. And, if none of these things happen, then black students are still victims of racism if the university they attend received, perhaps centuries ago, a donation from a philanthropist who made money from colonialism or slavery. At the same time, white students are taught about the problems with white privilege, white fragility and unintended microaggressions.

George, a professor from a London university, undertook anti-racism training at his institution:
'There are a whole bunch of committees that require you to have untaken diversity training prior to your appointment, and sitting on these committees is essential for career progression. So, in this respect, diversity

training is not really optional. I think this is the way it is across all universities. It's mandatory by stealth; they don't tell you explicitly that it's compulsory but you know that you have to do it, it's needed for every hoop you have to jump through.

'The training I undertook occurred before the wave of BLM protests last summer but it was driven by a similar form of political activism. We have quite an activist diversity committee at the institutional level and also at the school level and the people on these committees always have to be doing more. So the first thing might be decolonisation and they check to see how we are doing on that, and then the next thing might be all black studentships and after that it is diversity training. They're always trying to do more.

'The diversity training I attended was put on by a specialist company from outside of the university. There were two parts to it: we had to do online training first. This was much better in that, at very least, it wasn't so ideological. And then we had to do an in-person session. So to begin with we had to complete an online bias awareness course and we had to achieve a certain score. Then there was the workshop and they talked to us about the problems with our implicit attitudes. Anti-female discrimination was also a big topic. But there wasn't much substance behind it; for example, they would focus on a paper showing that women are discriminated against in higher education but they would ignore all the research that challenges this. They cherry pick the studies that make their argument and ignore all the rest. There was no scope for questioning any of this.

'Most of the participants in the workshop seemed

to agree with each other and with the people running the presentation. The atmosphere was one where you were clearly not expected to challenge anything that was said. It was certainly not conducive to debate. No one raised any critical questions, some people just kept their heads bowed, but generally it was all applauding the presenters, with some even encouraging them to go further in what they were saying.

'No one will say anything critical but my guess is that some of my colleagues would have at least a degree of scepticism about diversity training. But voicing this out loud could see you turned into a social pariah; you don't want people to think you are racist. Some departments at my university that have a much larger share of political radicals, but some departments are a little more heterodox. It seems to me that most academics are not really pushing for cancellations but on the other hand they are quite happy to support things like mandatory quotas for race and sex on course reading lists. So there is not a great deal of support for cancel culture but more radical academics are able to leverage the taboos of our age to amplify their power.

'There seems to be an underlying sacralisation of race and gender, as if these are the important categories. Anything people say must be accepted if the person speaking can claim membership of one of these totemic groups. No one is willing to challenge them because they have brought into this substructure of totemic beliefs where some groups are sacralised. Until we are able to say this is just one sociological category and there are other ways of grouping people we will always have this assumption that whenever a person of colour speaks they must be speaking the truth because they are from a holy category. People don't want to be on the wrong side of this. They might be in favour of academic freedom but they don't want to have to choose between academic freedom and social justice and so this means any claim on behalf of a marginalised group will always trump academic freedom. At heart this is a value conflict.

'There's a huge degree of conformity expected, driven in part by activists and in part by a bureaucracy that focuses on targets and charters like Athena Swan. These two things go hand in hand and together they are really aimed at bringing about wholesale change in the mission of the university. Activists want their values to be infused into every part of the institution. What's interesting is that these values do not always play out in practice, particularly when it comes to recruitment. When it comes down to the final decision, sometimes the diversity virtue signalling falls away and people resort to arguing, 'Well, we know this person.' This particularly seems to be the case if, for example, the person being interviewed is BAME or a woman but perhaps doesn't seem to hold the same opinions as the people doing the recruiting. The bottom line is that they would rather have someone with the right ideological credentials than someone who meets the diversity targets. We need to get political discrimination centred alongside and with an equal status to these other diversity issues. Every organisation has an ideological skew, so there is always political discrimination going on. If we said that, not academics, but the university administration had to be politically neutral, that would revolutionise the academy.'

One problem with the growth of anti-racism training in higher education is that it may perpetuate some of the problems it purports to remedy. Ruth Mieschbuehler argues that there is a real danger that campus relations at universities will become increasingly racialised. She uses the term 'racialisation' to refer to the process of emphasising racial and ethnic groups with the result that students are 'minoritised' and portrayed as needing differential treatment. For example, promoting the view that walking past a statue on campus is a source of psychological harm suggests black students are uniquely vulnerable and lacking in resilience. This assumption morphs into the patronising view that black students can only learn if they see themselves represented in the curriculum, in other words, that black students can only learn 'black knowledge' and are not capable of learning Kant or Shakespeare.

Through anti-racism campaigns and training, black students are often presented as an homogenous group but, in reality, the black Oxford student who has been privately educated and is from a wealthy family background probably shares few experiences in common with the black student who has grown up on a council estate and currently attends a lower ranking university while simultaneously holding down a part-time job. The presentation of all black students as victims of the past who continue to suffer racial discrimination in the present masks far more significant social class inequalities.

The authors of the UUK report, *Tackling Racial Harrassment in Higher Education*, suggest, 'It may be helpful to have separate spaces for Black, Asian and minority ethnic staff and students to discuss among themselves, as well as discussion forums for white students and staff.' Their recommendations end, it seems, in segregation.[86] Rather than promoting academic rigour and celebrating intellectual diversity, UUK employ contemporary anti-racism to shore up the moral authority of institutions that have become otherwise devoid of purpose. Unable to defend academic disciplines that stand accused of Eurocentrism or elitism, UUK fall back on shaping 'the minds and attitudes of the next generation' and 'driving cultural change'. Tragically, one consequence of this is the rehabilitation of racial divisions between staff and students on campus, up to and including segregation.

The Workplace

Racism is considered to be endemic within workplaces. It is assumed to be manifest in disparate access to the labour market and unequal opportunities within employment sectors, meaning BAME people are less likely to be employed, more likely to be in temporary or insecure work, and less likely to secure promotion to senior positions. At the same time, racism in the workplace is not in any way comparable to the formal barriers on employment legally enforceable only decades ago. It is also the case that, once again, not all BAME people have the same experiences in the workplace. Some groups, and many individuals, experience no barriers to their career progression or earnings. However, the position of professional anti-racists employed in the Human Resource departments of large companies, or diversity trainers who run staff development workshops, can only be maintained by pointing to – and purporting to be able to ameliorate – the continued existence of racism.

Binna Kandola, a Business Psychologist and the author of *Racism at Work*, describes how he sees the current situation:

'The racism in organisations today is not characterised by hostile abuse and threatening behaviour. It is not overt nor is it obvious. Today racism is subtle and nuanced, detected mostly by the people on the receiving end, but ignored and possibly not even seen by perpetrators and bystanders. Racism today may be more refined, but it harms people's careers and lives in hugely significant ways.'[87]

The form of racism being described here is so subtle people need to be trained to perceive it, yet so devastating it does irreparable damage to people's careers. Kandola explains this apparent contradiction by claiming, 'indifference is now the principal way in which racism is perpetuated in organisations.'[88]

Racism that hides behind indifference is difficult to identify. Kandola, having engaged with significant psychological research, detects this new form of racism in the things people do *not* say. Racism, he tells us, exists within people who, 'do not engage in expressing negative views about minority groups,' but actually, 'believe in greater integration,' and even individuals who, 'may consistently support policies that promote diversity'. Modern-day racism, Kandola informs us, hides behind the assumption that racial equality has been achieved, 'and that we need no further policies to promote equality.' To some, this may appear more like a political disagreement, or even simply a difference of approach to tackling social inequalities, but Kandola seems confident that he has uncovered one source of racism in the workplace.

Racism so subtle it exists only in what people do not say is explained by reference to the unconscious workings of our minds. According to Kandola, unconscious racism occurs because, 'The legacy of racist ideas, actions and imagery lives on publicly in stereotypes –and privately in our unconscious minds.' As will be explored more fully below, this brain-based historical legacy is a problem because, 'people with whom we interact pick up on and identify our unconscious behaviours.' This understanding of racism puts people in a bind: racism exists because of a past we cannot alter and it plays out in things we do not say. This suggests that racism will always be with us and there is little we can do to challenge it.

There are clearly racial discrepancies in access to and experiences of the labour market. Richard Norrie points out that in 2018, the overall unemployment rate was 4 per cent but that 'variation between ethnic groups ranged from 3 per cent for white minorities ('white Other') to 8 per cent of Bangladeshi/ Pakistanis and 9 per cent of black people.'[89] Research carried out by the TUC claims BAME employees are facing a triple hit of lower pay, temporary work and underemployment (unable to work as many hours as they would like).[90] One problem with such statistics is that they tell us little about how employment opportunities vary when ethnicity is correlated with sex, age, educational attainment and social class. If black people are more likely to be represented among the working class then, by definition, they will have lower paid and more insecure employment.

Clearly, this does not exclude the possibility of racial discrimination shaping people's life chances either before they seek employment or once in the workplace, but it does suggest that the complex nature of inequality means it is not simply resolvable with a brief diversity training seminar. Yet although contemporary anti-racists tell us that racism is systemic, they often remove discussion of solutions to problems of racial inequality away from the sphere of society and look only at individual psychology. This means that the focus for change is correcting the beliefs, attitudes and etiquette of individuals rather than collective campaigns for better employment rights. In focusing on informal networks that may operate in workplaces, professional anti-racists overlook the fact that, across society, people's attitudes towards race and racism have shifted enormously over several decades.

One route to furthering racial equality in the workplace may simply be to do nothing – as people become generally more tolerant, their social and professional networks naturally seem to expand. If diversity training is thought necessary, it could focus on encouraging people to expand their social networks and to be open to friendships with people who do not look like them. In contrast, a danger of focusing on individual attitudes is that this may not only make little difference to the employment prospects of black people but, worse, in racialising employers and promoting conscious – rather than spontaneous – interactions, it may make it more difficult for informal networks and friendships in the workplace to develop.

Kandola acknowledges that 'in-group bias, as opposed to out-group hostility [...] may account for the fact that minorities feel they do not receive, or have access to, development opportunities at work.' In other words, it is not that colleagues are prejudiced against minorities but that they show preference for people who appear more like them. As Kandola explains: 'When we are interacting with our in-group we are more altruistic and cooperative. We attribute success to the group's ability, and failures to other factors.' Yet much workplace diversity training focuses upon the benefits of differences between groups of people rather than stressing the similarities. We are expected to celebrate diversity, not what we have in common.

Prompting awareness about difference and stressing the need for huge sensitivity and an entirely new etiquette around dealing with people from diverse cultural backgrounds can lead to unintended consequences. Kandola suggests that:

'Minorities are less likely to receive immediate feedback, particularly when it is negative. [...] The lack of robust, constructive and supportive feedback may ensure that line managers avoid a potentially difficult conversation, but does little to help minorities improve their performance as early as possible.'

In this way, concern about issuing negative feedback for fear of breaching a particular protocol may stand in the way of a BAME employee's career progression.

The push for positive discrimination in both hiring and promoting BAME employees may also have unintended consequences. Underperformance by black members of staff may be overlooked if it is assumed they were an 'equity employee' or hired to fill a quota. Whereas a white member of staff may be encouraged to improve, a black member of staff may be left underperforming. By the same token, successful black employees may feel undermined if they come to believe others suspect them of having been promoted simply to meet a diversity target. Kandola labels the fact that 'our assessment of what other people think of us impacts not just our performance but our feelings and thoughts' as 'stereotype threat'.

Nonetheless, the number of corporate diversity and inclusion programmes is rising. The exact names and specific goals of such workshops vary, from helping to increase recruitment and retention of people from underrepresented groups, to eliminating prejudicial attitudes or behaviours, to reducing conflict and enhancing cooperation and teamwork among all employees.

Amanda is a director at a global accountancy firm:
'I am fortunate to work for an organisation that values diversity and wants to take direct action to address inequality. I have attended several different types of diversity programmes over the years. The most recent was the least formal. It was really just a conversation about race between colleagues. Gender came into it a little bit, but it was mainly about race. People were invited to talk about their experiences of being non-white and how this may have negatively impacted upon them. And some people's experiences were truly horrendous. I felt awful that they had been through this. Then there were other stories that made me wonder if what was being described really happened because of the person's race or whether other factors, for example their age, might be a more plausible explanation. But it didn't really feel appropriate to challenge anything anyone said. One of my black colleagues told me after the discussion that she felt under pressure to contribute and this made her feel uncomfortable.

'I think the point was to make us empathise with people who are not white and have a different experience of situations many of us take for granted. I do think this could be a very important exercise. We are a large organisation and have a responsibility to do the right thing, to have a social conscience, to recruit a diverse workforce and to make sure there are no barriers in place preventing colleagues from progressing. But recently it can feel that diversity really means skin colour or gender, and other important elements of diversity, thought, background or socio-economic diversity, less so.

'We also watched a short video about the importance of being anti-racist. I did feel a little bit as if I had to start seeing my colleagues according to skin colour which I hadn't done before. I worried that I'd perhaps unwittingly said things that might offend in the past without even knowing it. It definitely makes you more anxious and more cautious about what you say. You can easily become quite self-conscious. And perhaps this is a good thing. We should be aware of what we say and how it might offend people but the downside of this is that it can make us more wary. Sometimes I think I'd far rather say nothing than risk saying the wrong thing and worrying that I might lose my job.

'Personally, I don't want to be seen as a woman first and a colleague second. I worked really hard to get where I am and my sex is irrelevant to this. It has never been a barrier to my progression. We need a level playing field and we need access but when this pushes over into quotas it takes away the idea of meritocracy, I don't want extra points because of something I have no control over. And I don't want others to think my sex helped me get a role or a promotion. Diversity is of critical importance, but diversity needs to include people with different viewpoints, people from different backgrounds, particularly socioeconomic, not just a focus on skin colour or sex. Socioeconomic inequality is widening, particularly with the pandemic, and that should be something we are all fighting to address. I'd like to see the proportion of people recruited or taken on as interns who come from homes below the poverty line.'

One of the main criticisms levelled at workplace diversity training programmes is that they simply do not work. If we accept the primary assumption of the race experts, that racism is systemic and deeply entrenched, then it is unlikely to be rectified with a one-off training session. However, other criticisms go far beyond diversity training simply not working.

Our historical and cultural knowledge means that older adults are aware of once-prevalent racial stereotypes even if they now know them to be outdated and wrong. Being aware of stereotypes does not mean that people agree with them or even recall them within their day-to-day interactions. Many diversity training sessions begin by asking participants to highlight stereotypes once associated with particular groups before discussing their damaging impact. Yet the act of asking people to rehearse stereotypes in this way may have the perverse consequence of reinforcing long-buried cliches and insults as well as potentially teaching a younger generation old fashioned attitudes. Whatever the intended outcome, the upshot can be to make all participants feel uncomfortable and pitch ethnic groups against one another. Likewise, many diversity training programmes present prejudice and discrimination as rampant which may have the unintended consequence of normalising bias.

Alternatively, organising and compelling attendance at anti-racism training sessions may leave managers to assume that equality and diversity have been 'done' and normal business can resume with no further issues needing to be considered. Those who subsequently raise concerns may find managers unreceptive to reopening a problem considered solved. Problems with diversity training may be exacerbated when attendance is made mandatory. Musa al-Gharbi argues:

'Mandatory training causes people to engage with the materials and exercises in the wrong frame of mind: adversarial and resentful. Consequently, mandatory training often leads to more negative feelings and behaviors, both towards the company and minority co-workers.'[91]

Online diversity training

Online diversity training is a growing enterprise with numerous virtual learning specialists providing modules that can be undertaken remotely, for certification, by individuals either of their own volition or as part of a company programme. The benefit for employers of this approach is that they can prove their staff have undergone training without entire teams being taken off task at the same time. For this reason, online training may prove more cost effective than bringing in outside speakers to host workshops. Alternatively, individuals may sign up to such courses in order to make themselves more employable with up-to-date knowledge and skills. Several online diversity training workshops are freely available for anyone to join. Although there are many different providers of online diversity training programmes, most follow a similar format. They comprise short, often animated, video clips followed by multiple choice questions for participants to complete. Content is often quite generic with a need to avoid specific issues that may not apply to all circumstances.

Grovo offers 'microlearning content on a platform that does the hard work for you,' with '2500+ lessons at the ready to help employees thrive'.[92] The lessons on diversity focus on encouraging people to 'collaborate across working styles'. It falls to the accompanying visuals to make clear, albeit implicitly, that 'working styles' is a euphemism for differences of race, sex and age. The starting point for the online lesson is that diversity is an asset; having team members with a range of working styles brings a range of benefits to a company.

It is assumed that 'It can be overwhelming working with new people from varied backgrounds'. Here, Grovo makes similar assumptions to other online diversity training providers: both young new recruits and older employees alike will be unlikely to have worked closely alongside, or even had much contact with, people who are not like them. No evidence is provided to substantiate this claim. Further assumptions are grounded in popular psychology: 'collaboration will come more naturally to you with some colleagues'. The emphasis throughout is on 'work styles and personality types' meaning that 'diversity of age, race, and gender' come to be equated with 'psychological traits like values, abilities, and working styles'.

This broader definition of diversity may be considered helpful, particularly if it extends to tolerance for viewpoint diversity. The danger, however, is that age, race and gender come to be intrinsically associated with certain psychological traits and values. At best, this may lead managers to believe they have 'done' diversity by putting together people who look different but think the same. At worst, the equation of physical characteristics with mental attributes may reinforce stereotypes. Nonetheless, the conclusion Grovo's participants are expected to reach is that 'working with people who are different from us leads us to approach tasks and problems in new, more productive ways' and therefore, 'diversity is not a drawback but an asset'. The multiple-choice format for assessment leaves little room for nuanced discussion of these points.

Coursera is a US-based, international provider of Massive Open Online Courses that operates in conjunction with over 200 'leading universities and companies' including Google, IBM, Imperial College London, and Stanford University. Coursera's Diversity and Inclusion in the Workplace programme is run by ESSEC Business School.[93] It comprises a series of mini lectures, delivered by a real lecturer (as opposed to an animated figure) with visual aids including graphs and charts. The aim is for participants to become 'familiar with diversity and inclusion issues in the workplace, understanding cognitive processes that fuel diversity dynamics, and developing reflexive reactions to these cognitive processes in order to develop your inclusive capabilities.' The emphasis on 'cognitive processes' indicates that psychology (rather than, say, sociology, politics or law) provides the theoretical context for the lessons provided. There is an emphasis on understanding and overcoming the role of the unconscious in relation to implicit biases people might hold. Again, the one-way nature of online delivery means discussion is impossible and interaction is limited to multiple choice questions. In this way, contested statements are presented as 'facts', substantiated by scientific evidence from the field of psychology, with right and wrong answers.

Future Learn is another global virtual learning provider. Its course *Understanding Diversity and Inclusion* is run in conjunction with Purdue University and aims to help participants, 'develop your attitudes, skills and knowledge of cultural diversity so you're able to create inclusive environments.'[94] Here, cultural diversity is presented as a body of knowledge – presumably, facts about different cultures – as well as an attitude and a set of skills. Assessment entails demonstrations of the 'correct' attitudes. The blurb for the course goes further in defining cultural diversity: 'Many things contribute to an individual's identity, including race, ethnicity, gender, age, appearance, religion, gender identity, sexual orientation, education, and political beliefs.' It is unusual to see acknowledgement of political beliefs as a feature of a person's identity; although the potential contradiction between tolerating different political beliefs and demonstrating correct attitudes towards cultural diversity is not acknowledged.

The course goes on to cover 'unconscious biases' and 'ethnocentric and ethno-relative mindsets'. A person with an ethnocentric mindset judges other cultures solely by the values and standards of their own culture. A person with an ethnorelative mindset, on the other hand, believes that no one culture is superior to any other. In one section of the course, participants are asked to 'select a diversity or difference that is unknown, confusing, or one you may avoid when possible. List a few reasons for your reaction.' The aim seems to be to make explicit people's unconscious biases for later examination.

Online courses are a cost-effective way for individuals and employers to undertake diversity training. Participants are more distanced from the subject matter under discussion than they would be in face-to-face workshops and there is more of a focus on correct answers to specific questions rather than more nuanced discussions. This can mean a greater emphasis on facts rather than the trainer's own viewpoint. It also seems to mean a more general approach that encompasses a broader range of issues, such as political diversity. The online courses I reviewed appeared to steer clear of more controversial issues such as white privilege or white fragility. However, common assumptions such as biological diversity equating to viewpoint diversity, and the existence of and need to examine unconscious biases, are reinforced. The danger is that participants expend time and effort simply learning to recite platitudes.

Unconscious bias

Almost all diversity training today seems driven by the assumption that people have implicit attitudes or unconscious biases. The existence of such biases is often taken as an article of faith although one that can be measured through implicit association tests and detected in brain scans. Kandola explains: 'Certain parts of the brain have been implicated in the process of prejudice and bias, namely the amygdala, the ventromedial prefrontal cortex (VmPFC) and the insular cortex.' This lends scientific, if not ethical, credibility to unconscious bias training. That we act out our unconscious biases, to the detriment of particular groups, is also assumed to be simply common sense. The role of the trainer is to make conscious the workings of our unconscious brain, subject its contents to scrutiny, and teach us how to compensate for our unconscious through better conscious action.

The non-judgmental starting point of diversity training is that 'we all have unconscious bias'. Indeed, not only do we all have unconscious bias but – the very fact that this bias is located within our unconscious – means it is beyond our control. We are relieved of all responsibility for what may be found in our unconscious. It has been put there by society and culture; through our upbringing, education, interactions with the media and other people. It is assumed that we act out our unconscious thoughts and are nudged by our biases, without being aware that this is what we are doing.

Proof of unconscious bias comes from implicit association tests that aim to track our response times when asked to match certain images, words or phrases with people of different characteristics. As Kandola explains, the theory is that 'our response times will be quicker and more accurate when the characteristics we are judging match more closely with our cognitive schemas.' In other words: 'Participants found it easier to associate black people with negative words and achievements than with positive ones.' This is said to be due to the persistence of cultural stereotypes that are deeply rooted within our brains and influence our ways of thinking. Even though we may not acknowledge holding any prejudicial thoughts towards certain groups, and may not act in a prejudicial way, we may still harbour prejudices without knowing it: 'Our overt behaviours and expressed attitudes may be egalitarian and tolerant, but our implicit attitudes may be the opposite.'

Kandola argues that one cause of implicit biases is that people have 'limited direct personal experience of minority group members' and 'constructive intergroup interactions'. This means that 'most of their information about other groups [is] obtained from the media' and so they 'develop unconscious negative associations.' However, rather than allowing people to gain personal experience through informal interactions, Kandola concludes that, 'The key here is to give the person feedback on their behaviour and give them the opportunity to learn.' His solution to the problem of unconscious bias is to circumvent people's agency to act on their own volition in the workplace through the implementation of a framework of very explicit norms. He suggests the danger of not adopting this approach is that 'residual feelings will rise to the surface and lead to more discriminatory behaviour.'

Microsoft offers an 'eLesson' in unconscious bias.[95] The starting point is to normalise unconscious bias and to absolve people of responsibility for their own biases:

'People can be biased about just about anything — not just things like gender, skin color, or age, but also things like communication style or what someone does in their free time. Unconscious bias is not intentional — it's part of the lens through which we see the world.'

'Biases are shortcuts our brain forms based on:

- our own experiences
- things other people tell us
- media portrayals
- institutional influences
- other external influences

'No matter how well-meaning we are, we are all susceptible to bias. It's our brains' way of making sense of the flood of information that is coming at us constantly.'

Microsoft is clear that the problem with making sense of the world in this way is that:

'when people don't fit our internalized expectations, we can sometimes have difficulty seeing their talents, motivations, and potential clearly — which can mean we interact with them less effectively.'

Fortunately, with considerable effort and repeated practice, Microsoft is confident that we can reduce the impact of our unconscious bias:

'Because our unconscious biases are so hidden from ourselves, it takes some work to disrupt them, but it can be done through active reflection and practicing inclusive behaviors. Doing this work benefits us, the people around us, and our business.'

The intended outcome of the eLesson is that:

'you'll deepen your understanding of unconscious biases, how they influence behavior, and how they impact us all. You'll also learn numerous actions you can take to help counter bias in your own work environment.'

Tom is an IT professional:
'The last company I worked for ran a diversity training workshop a few weeks after the killing of George Floyd in America and following the Black Lives Matter protests. But the company was clearly thinking along these lines already and anti-racism had become a major focus of its work. There might have been an opportunistic sense that this was good PR, but I do think they genuinely believed in what they were doing. They went to a great deal of effort.

'It was assumed that diversity training would be a good thing for us all to do. No one really questioned it. The general day-to-day conversation could be quite political; some people were very vocal in sharing their views about President Trump or Brexit. They just seemed to assume that they were right and everyone agreed with them.

'An external company was brought in to run the diversity training we had. It really seemed to be a campaigning organisation that makes money from running workshops. They had quite a generic presentation that had no doubt been used elsewhere. We were not told in advance what to expect, but we were reminded that attendance was compulsory. I didn't want to rock the boat and question it and I was curious to find out what it was all about.

'The training was held virtually because we were under lockdown at the time. It began with a lecture and an introduction to the ground rules. We were told that we were in a safe space and that there was not to be any racism or sexism of any kind whatsoever. There was the proviso 'not that we expect any' but it did feel like they clearly felt the need to tell us off. But at the same time we were told we had to keep an open mind throughout! This same, very forceful, tone was used at the end of the session too.

'They had clearly put a lot of effort into organising the presentation, it was very professional and well structured. One section was on different types of racism. They told us that the dictionary definition of racism was not good enough and that it needed to be expanded. They then showed us the dictionary definition of racism and asked us if we thought it was good enough. But they had already told us the answer they expected and so this made it virtually impossible to question anything that was said. But people went along with it, they answered the question, they said the dictionary definition is not good enough.

'They worked hard to keep our attention, to get us to engage. But the only way we could participate was to enter comments in the chat function. So people said what was expected of them and the trainers read these messages out. We had sections on unconscious bias and white privilege but it all mainly followed the same format of them telling us the right answers before asking questions to check we had understood.

'There was one bit in particular that really stuck in my mind. They said that in the past there were laws that discriminated against black people, which is true, but then they said, some aspects of these laws are still in effect today. This struck me as just wrong. They extrapolated from something that was true into something that wasn't true at all. But there were no opportunities to question this. It seemed unnecessarily confrontational.

> 'There was no way of knowing what most people thought about what was being said. It was only weeks later that a colleague told me he hated it just as much as I did. We both said it should never have been made mandatory. Personally, I think we should just keep politics out of the workplace. Some members of staff are able to dominate discussions during work time with no respect for the fact that not everyone agrees with them. There is a lack of consideration and awareness and sensitivity to people with different political views.'

There are several criticisms to be levelled at both the idea of unconscious bias and diversity training that purports to compensate for our biases. The idea that our unconscious can be readily accessed with a brain scanning machine or revealed to us through a rapid-fire computer test is highly contested. For unconscious bias to result in discriminatory practices, we must assume a direct link between our implicit attitudes and our behaviour. Yet research has shown that implicit attitudes do not effectively predict actual discriminatory behavior.[96] This suggests either that unconscious biases cannot be accurately measured, or, that people are able to exercise a degree of control over their speech or actions and do not automatically and straightforwardly act out the contents of their unconscious mind.

We also need to consider the morality and efficacy of seeking to change our unconscious minds. Musa al-Gharbi, writing at *Heterodox Academy*, argues that:

> 'most interventions to change implicit attitudes are ineffective (effects, when present, tend to be small and fleeting). Moreover, there is no evidence that changing implicit attitudes has any significant, let alone durable, impact on reducing biased or discriminatory behaviors.'[97]

Ethically, unconscious bias training could be considered just a waste of time if it is ineffective. However, pseudo-scientific claims to be revealing the inner workings of our brain, in the workplace and in a context of racism being one of the biggest sins a person can commit, are far worse than simply a waste of time. They cross a boundary that breaches the rights of an individual to freedom of conscience. Furthermore, unconscious bias training may actually harm relationships between colleagues. It pushes people to see each other as members of a racial group in ways they may not have done previously and, in a bid to make all interactions conscious, it risks preventing the spontaneity and informality that leads to genuine friendship.

Microaggressions

As legal discrimination has been abolished and all forms of explicit racism, whether from institutions or individuals, have become socially unacceptable, anti-racism campaigners have turned their attention to microagressions. The term 'microaggression' was originally coined by Chester M. Pierce in 1970 to describe the casual insults and dismissals he noticed white Americans aiming at African Americans. However, it is really in the past five years that the term has entered everyday dialogue.

Anti-racist campaigners argue that the prohibition on expressing racist views in the open does not mean that racism has gone away but that attitudes are expressed in a 'micro' format. Kandola defines workplace incivility as 'low intensity acts which violate the norms of respectful behaviours established in a specific setting, and whose intent to harm is ambiguous.' He continues:

> 'Micro-incivilities are the kinds of daily, commonplace behaviours or aspects of an environment which signal,

wittingly or unwittingly, to members of outgroups that they do not belong and are not welcome. They include subtle slights or insults that are, in some respects, products of the automatic ways in which we respond to out-groups.'

Indeed, as Kandola explains, the microaggression may not be an action or an utterance at all, 'but an absence or a withholding.' In this way, everything from facial expressions to not making eye contact with someone can be considered a racial microaggression. Other types of omission that might be considered examples of microaggression include: not sitting facing a person; not giving someone your attention; persistently not saying someone's name correctly and not inviting someone to speak up in a meeting.

So slight are the aggressions and insults that one role of the anti-racism trainer is to enable people to detect microaggressions they may not otherwise have noticed. Much anti-racism training aims to raise awareness of both the nature and impact of microaggressions on people of colour. A key message is that the psychological impact of microaggressions is cumulative over time and leads to the erosion of self-confidence. Often, instruction in microaggressions follows lessons on unconscious bias and a link is drawn between the two: it is because of our unconscious biases that we unintentionally mistreat people who are different to ourselves.

There are a number of criticisms to be made of anti-racism training designed to counter microaggressions. There is a lack of substantive evidence that such training brings about long-term changes in participants' behaviour. Neither can it be proven that such training results in institutional changes such as more recruitment and better promotion prospects for BAME people. However, it may be the case that training in microaggressions actually has a negative impact on equality.

One reason for this lies in the mismatch between the nature of the microaggression and the rhetoric employed to describe its impact. The actions under discussion are, for example, a failure to make eye contact or asking someone where they come from, yet the impact is discussed in terms of psychological harm. Training and awareness raising around microaggressions teaches BAME people to find offence in slights they may otherwise have brushed off or not even noticed. It then tells them that the cumulative impact of these slights will cause them long-lasting damage. Musa al-Gharbi argues:

'we have ample reason to believe that sensitizing people to perceive and take greater offense at these slights actually *would* cause harm: the evidence is clear and abundant that increased perceptions of racism have adverse mental and physical consequences for minorities.'[98]

At the same time as BAME people are taught to perceive offence, white people are taught that not only their speech but their body language and eye movements may reveal a deeply hidden racism. The only way to counteract this, white people are taught, is to be hyper-vigilant in their every interaction. This complicates and problematises spontaneous relationships. Musa al-Gharbi argues that:

'By calling attention, not just to clear examples of harm and prejudice, but just as much (or more) to things like implicit attitudes and microaggressions, participants come to view colleagues from historically marginalized and disenfranchised groups as fragile and easily offended. As a result, members of the dominant group become less likely to try to build relationships or collaborate with people from minority populations.'

It may make people retreat from forging the informal connections that often lead to opportunities for promotion.

It may also make managers less likely to offer feedback to employees that lead to better performance. In short, microaggression training does little to solve problems in the workplace but may create new problems by racialising employees and encouraging hyper-sensitivity and vigilance in all interactions.

Active bystander training

Active bystander training (sometimes called allyship training) builds on the theory of microaggressions. It aims to teach and empower colleagues to intervene if they witness racism in the workplace. It is assumed that all forms of racism, including microaggressions and microincivilities, inflict a devastating psychological blow upon those who experience them. But, unlike unconscious bias training which focuses on the unwitting perpetrators of racism, or microaggression workshops which often focus on the feelings of the victims, active bystander training considers the role of witnesses. The starting point is that, in failing to act or speak out, witnesses compound the pain inflicted by the original act.

Through active bystander training, people can be given 'the skills to challenge unacceptable behaviours, including those which may have become normalised over time.' Specific skills taught include: overcoming fear and paralysis in challenging situations; using the right words and expressions when challenging behaviours; tackling 'micro-inequities', including eye-rolling, sighing, constant interruptions and unconscious bias.[99]

Participants in active bystander training will be taught particular ways to intervene and act if they are witness to racism. One training provider aims to instruct people in 'The 4D's'. This includes lessons in: how to take direct action to shut down debates and arguments by using words and body language to show disapproval and make it more difficult for people to interrupt; how to distract protagonists, defuse awkward situations and create positive culture change; how to delegate by reporting unacceptable behaviours and escalating problems with integrity; and finally, how to take advantage of a delay to your intervention.

Sandra works in the HR department of a national company:
'The diversity workshops we run in this country seem to be a lot less confrontational than the ones that are held elsewhere, particularly in the US. It seems to me that we prefer to take a softer, more therapeutic approach to these issues. We really try very hard not to alienate people. But, at times, this can mean that there's a temptation to shy away from just saying what needs to be said. Even when I first attended an equality and diversity workshop over twenty years ago now, those running it tended to avoid simply saying, 'this is the law, this is what it means to discriminate against someone, and this is what will happen to you if you do.'

'Back then, it seemed that there was much more of an idea that you could run a diversity training and that was it; job done. You wouldn't need to put the same group of people through that training again. Things have really moved on since then. Today it is much more likely to be assumed that because we all have unconscious bias then it is worth attending some kind of workshop or training far more regularly so you can keep your biases in check.

'The company I work for tries to take a far more

holistic approach to diversity and inclusion. Rather than simply running one-off training sessions we try to look at the entire workplace culture. For example, we hold focus groups with people from a similar background or with a shared identity and these groups will regularly feedback to managers. People choose to join these groups and certain employees really seem to like going along and being part of this.

'Generally, we try to operate a forgiving culture. The assumption is that staff members are fundamentally good and trying to do the right thing but may inadvertently say something that could upset someone else. The message is that we shouldn't be defensive about this, you just need to work out where your biases have come from. Your biases are more likely to come out when you are not on your guard. So we try to get people to have honest but sympathetic conversations with each other and without getting people's defences up.

'We do still have more formal training on offer too. The last one I went on was all about being an ally. The idea is that if you see or hear something you think is wrong then you should speak up and challenge it. If it happened to you then you should feel able to tell people how you feel. So we are all very much encouraged to talk to each other directly about any issues that might arise but there is an assumption that our conversations will follow a particular formula. At times I get a little concerned that people might become deskilled and be left not knowing how to have normal conversations with each other.

'The last time I did this training it was delivered virtually because of the pandemic. We split into breakout rooms online and were given scenarios to play out and discuss. The focus was really on how we get on with each other and create an inclusive workplace so we can all be happy at work. As I work in HR, we are expected to act as role models in relation to equality and diversity. People don't really think about why they are doing these things, this is just the job nowadays, this is what we are doing all the time. But at the end of the day it is still quite a powerful thing. It's a means of overseeing and intervening in staff relationships.

'At the same time, it can seem as if most people are not hugely ideologically committed to the ideas being promoted. Many people seem to be going through the motions. This means there can be a disconnectedness. We have phrases like 'corporate social responsibility' ticking away in the background, like little stickers we have to put on, but everyone knows that the company's main business is elsewhere.'

There are problems specific to active bystander training. It again serves to racialise workplaces by encouraging people to see each other as members of distinct groups. It reinforces the notion that everyday experiences that are part and parcel of human interaction may be acts of aggression when carried out by white people and cause psychological harm to people of colour. There is a further danger that active bystander training may infantilise BAME people by institutionalising an expectation that they will be unable to deal with difficult situations or colleagues themselves and will need other people to speak up on their behalf.

Conclusions

Diversity and anti-racism training has become the norm in schools, universities and the workplace. The most common forms of diversity training are grounded in Critical Race Theory. This shows that far from posing a radical challenge to the status quo, CRT is now the established approach to anti-racism. Yet such an approach rehabilitates old prejudices and creates new problems. Much of the thinking, and many of the leading proponents of CRT, come from the US. Yet often its ideas are imported wholesale into the UK and other countries without considering their specific historical and cultural context. For example, Britain had no equivalent of enforced segregation but citizens arriving in the UK from former-colonies did experience racial discrimination and prejudice. This is at best misunderstood and at worst ignored if we superimpose an American analytical framework onto British society. However, this does not stop the diversity juggernaut from ploughing on: producing more publications, devising new courses, entering new workplaces. In fact, just as with the broader cultural dissemination of therapeutic practice, so too do we now have the mainstreaming of the ideas and practices that underpin diversity training in all walks of life.

Today's anti-racism training starts from the premise that racism is deeply entrenched within society and intrinsic to our personal identity. As Kendi explains, 'We are surrounded by racial inequity, as visible as the law, as hidden as our private thoughts.' This denies all progress towards equality that has been made and suggests attempts at further change will be futile. Renni Eddo-Lodge does not see the increase in inter-racial families as a positive sign that people are becoming less prejudiced. Instead, she argues that 'white privilege is never more pronounced than in our intimate relationships, our close friendships and our families,' and urges parents of mixed-race children, 'to be humble, and to learn that they are racist even if they don't think that they are.'[100]

CRT insists that everyone has a racial identity and that this alone determines our perception and understanding of the world. It emphasises differences rather than similarities between people and rejects colour-blindness in favour of us all being encouraged to view each other as racialized beings. As a result, anti-racism becomes reduced to a quest for examples to expose the racism that has already been determined to exist. A focus on microaggressions, for example, may well surprise people who came up against legal discriminatory policies in employment and housing several decades ago. Yet, to DiAngelo, 'racism's adaptations over time are more sinister than concrete rules such as Jim Crow.'[101] The emphasis on group membership simultaneously erodes both differences between individuals and the possibility of finding common cause across identity groupings. In rehashing stereotypes that have long been challenged, CRT breathes life back into racial thinking. At worst, this provides fresh justification for racial segregation. For example, the Universities UK briefing, *Tackling racial harassment in higher education* advises: 'It may be helpful to have separate spaces for Black, Asian and minority ethnic staff and students to discuss among themselves, as well as discussion forums for white students and staff.'

In contrast to the civil rights era, anti-racism has moved from aiming to eradicate race to seeing everyone as racialised; from considering racism an aberration to viewing it as the norm. The search for solutions has shifted from a focus on the material conditions of people's lives to the inner workings of their minds; from challenging legal inequalities to calling-out cultural representations. In this way, the rise of CRT intersects with the growth of victim culture and the transformation of politics into therapy thwarts demands for material change. CRT's obsession with racial categorisation and white privilege leaves little room to consider the impact of social class on people's life chances. Indeed, in the rush to construct intersectional hierarchies that position people of colour as oppressed victims of entrenched white superiority, the experiences of wealthy, highly educated, well-connected black people are overlooked. And rather than promoting solidarity between working class people of all skin colours, poor white people must be taught to recognise their original sin.

CRT asks us to focus on 'white fragility' as an explanation for the discomfort white people express when accused of being racist. Yet the very fact of expressing discomfort at such accusations suggests that far from being a cultural norm, racist attitudes are considered shameful nowadays. Ironically, although the focus is on white fragility, CRT promotes black victimhood. Black people are never permitted to forget that they are victims of historical injustices and continued oppression in the present. Just as white people are taught to check their privilege, so too are black people taught to recognise their victimhood. Kendi explains why he no longer uses the term 'microaggression':

'A persistent daily low hum of racist abuse is not minor. I use the term 'abuse' because aggression is not as exacting a term. Abuse accurately describes the action and its effects on people: distress, anger, worry, depression, anxiety, pain, fatigue and suicide.'[102]

Here we see that black people are not only taught how to interpret their daily experiences but are also instructed in the correct emotional responses to such interactions. Symptomatic of this approach is the rejection of free speech as a weapon in tackling instances of racism. Nowhere is it suggested that the best solution to racial slights or demonstrations of white fragility might be informal dialogue between the various parties. A brief conversation between offender and offendee may resolve interpersonal conflicts before they develop further. But such simplistic solutions would leave an army of race professionals from human resource managers to diversity trainers without employment. Instead, people are warned of the dangers of spontaneous interactions:

'The idea that one can use words to undo the meanings that others attach to these very same words is to commit the empathic fallacy—the belief that one can change a narrative by merely offering another, better one—that the reader's or listener's empathy will quickly and reliably take over.'[103]

Such statements illustrate the contemptuous view critical race theorists hold of the public. They also reveal how, when authority over workplace relations is delegated to race experts, the required deference makes solidarity between workers impossible.

Anti-racism training creates a dependency upon the same experts that sow division. The ranks of the race experts have expanded to encompass the wider graduate class of knowledge workers, bureaucrats and managers, who have imbibed the CRT script. They know the correct vocabulary to use and attitudes to express to differentiate their enlightened anti-racism from the more retrograde attitudes of others. They know that three years ago, the acronym BME (Black and Minority Ethnic) fell out of fashion and was replaced by BAME (with Asian specified) and now, BAME itself is on its way out. Such special insights into white privilege and the impact of microaggressions allow them to justify their position but transform anti-racism into an exclusive – not inclusive – enterprise.

Not only is anti-racism training widely available today, it is often mandatory for workers, students or pupils, or becomes effectively mandatory under pressure from peers and managers. When such training requirements are made in the absence of any specific complaint or issue to resolve, attendance becomes a means to promote a particular political outlook. This means that public and private companies, as well as educational institutions have, through diversity training, power to subject people to an ideology they may not otherwise choose to buy into. What's more, the potential to raise disagreements is rarely a feature of diversity training sessions. Indeed, as the UK chair of KPMG discovered in February 2021, voicing disagreements with the central tenets of anti-racism training, such as unconscious bias, can lead to public humiliation and end a career. Bill Michael said in a virtual staff meeting: 'There is no such thing as unconscious bias, I don't buy it. Because after every single unconscious bias training that has ever been done, nothing's ever improved.'[104] Although he issued an immediate apology, KPMG launched an independent investigation into Michael's comments. He subsequently resigned before the outcome was announced.

Despite his position becoming untenable, Michael's statement that unconscious bias training leads to few practical improvements is not only accurate, the same can also be said of most anti-racism training programmes.

> 'An empirical literature was built up measuring the effectiveness of diversity-related training programs. The picture that has emerged is not very flattering. In a nutshell, it seems that these training programs generally fail at their stated goals, and often produce unfortunate and unintended consequences.'[105]

The ineffectiveness of such training programmes appears to be no barrier to their popularity or the fees their purveyors can charge. Writing on *Minding the Campus*, Robert Maranto notes: 'Profit-seeking prophets promote their ventures as a way of warding off charges of racism and as a defense against lawsuits, no matter an organization's actual treatment of the disadvantaged.'[106] Whether through cowardice, calculation or conviction, it certainly seems easier for employers and managers to hold diversity training sessions than to consider factors such as social class which still have a considerable impact upon social mobility and equal opportunity. Yet the tragic consequence is that racial divisions are becoming ever more firmly entrenched.

Recommendations

1. Education and training are two distinct things. No school pupil or university student should be taught CRT as fact, have to undergo mandatory unconscious bias training, or be compelled to attend any other form of anti-racism training.

2. No employee should face losing their job for refusing to undertake workplace anti-racism training or for raising legitimate concerns with the content of such training programmes.

3. An inquiry should be held into the soliciting, investigating and recording of non-crime hate incidents. The gathering of statistics relating to such incidents has become open to exploitation by activists. Data is used to legitimise a sense of victimhood among minority communities and lend weight to the concept of microaggression.

4. Reassert the importance of equality before the law. Workplace training sessions could play a useful role in informing employees about legal duties not to discriminate.

5. Positive discrimination should be exceptional and only take place under specific and limited circumstances. In such instances where positive discrimination is deemed necessary, a candidate's social class background should be considered alongside race and sex.

6. Schools, universities and workplaces should be encouraged to place greater value upon viewpoint diversity, rather than just biological diversity, and what people have in common, rather than simply what divides us.

Notes

1   Police force warns cops who don't kneel at BLM rallies they may be targeted
2   Harry and Meghan Have Also Been Supporting Black Lives Matter in Britain
3   Premier League players to wear 'Black Lives Matter' on back of shirts
4   Here are the retailers going beyond solidarity for Black Lives Matter
5   Silence Is NOT An Option
6   https://uk.gofundme.com/f/ukblm-fund
7   Revealed: What 'Black Lives Matter' really stands for
8   https://blacklivesmatter.com/about/
9   History of the hashtag #BlackLivesMatter: Social activism on Twitter
10 Michael Brown: the founding myth of Black Lives Matter
11 There Is No Epidemic of Fatal Police Shootings Against Unarmed Black Americans
12 Stop pretending the BLM protests were peaceful
13 https://blacklivesmatter.com/about/
14 Why is the UK government suddenly targeting 'critical race theory'? | Daniel Trilling
15 WEB Du Bois on Black 'Double-Consciousness'
16 Martin Luther King I Have a Dream Speech
17 Delgado, R. and Stefancic, J. (2017) *Critical Race Theory* (3rd Edition) NYU Press.
18 Mari J. Matsuda, Charles R. Lawrence III, Richard Delgado, Kimberle Williams Crenshaw, (1993) *Words That Wound, Critical Race Theory, Assaultive Speech, and the First Amendment*, Westview Press.
19 Delgado, R. and Stefancic, J. (2017) *Critical Race Theory* (3rd Edition) NYU Press.
20 Bell, D. (1987) cited in: Helen Pluckrose and James Lindsay, (2020) *Cynical Theories, How activist scholarship made everything about race, gender and identity*, Pitchstone Publishing.

21 Ibram X Kendi, (2019) *How to be an antiracist*, Bodley Head.
22 Ibram X Kendi, (2019) *How to be an antiracist*, Bodley Head.
23 Ibram X Kendi, (2019) *How to be an antiracist*, Bodley Head.
24 Ibram X Kendi, (2019) *How to be an antiracist*, Bodley Head.
25 Mari J. Matsuda, Charles R. Lawrence III, Richard Delgado, Kimberle Williams Crenshaw, (1993) *Words That Wound, Critical Race Theory, Assaultive Speech, and the First Amendment*, Westview Press.
26 Delgado, R. and Stefancic, J. (2017) *Critical Race Theory* (3rd Edition) NYU Press.
27 Delgado, R. and Stefancic, J. (2017) *Critical Race Theory* (3rd Edition) NYU Press.
28 Mari J. Matsuda, Charles R. Lawrence III, Richard Delgado, Kimberle Williams Crenshaw, (1993) *Words That Wound, Critical Race Theory, Assaultive Speech, and the First Amendment*, Westview Press.
29 Delgado, R. and Stefancic, J. (2017) *Critical Race Theory* (3rd Edition) NYU Press.
30 Mari J. Matsuda, Charles R. Lawrence III, Richard Delgado, Kimberle Williams Crenshaw, (1993) *Words That Wound, Critical Race Theory, Assaultive Speech, and the First Amendment*, Westview Press.
31 Mari J. Matsuda, Charles R. Lawrence III, Richard Delgado, Kimberle Williams Crenshaw, (1993) *Words That Wound, Critical Race Theory, Assaultive Speech, and the First Amendment*, Westview Press.
32 Robin DiAngelo, (2018) *White Fragility, Why it's so hard for white people to talk about race*, Penguin Random House.
33 Ibram X Kendi, (2019) *How to be an antiracist*, Bodley Head.
34 Ibram X Kendi, (2019) *How to be an antiracist*, Bodley Head.
35 In Mari J. Matsuda, Charles R. Lawrence III, Richard Delgado, Kimberle Williams Crenshaw, (1993) *Words That Wound, Critical Race Theory, Assaultive Speech, and the First Amendment*, Westview Press.
36 https://nymag.com/intelligencer/2020/07/antiracism-training-white-fragility-robin-diangelo-ibram-kendi.html?fbclid=IwAR2UmwfpPeaYu5aOfcfeuDsF1ZPSWosi9HHvc7umPrXlsxI2l-tU_oGJQYZY
37 Delgado, R. and Stefancic, J. (2017) *Critical Race Theory* (3rd Edition) NYU Press.
38 Delgado, R. and Stefancic, J. (2017) *Critical Race Theory* (3rd Edition) NYU Press.
39 The New York Times Revises The 1619 Project, Barely by Peter Wood | NAS
40 Wood, P. (2020) 1620: A Critical Response to the 1619 Project, Encounter Books.

41 History GCSE to be given Black Lives Matter makeover

42 University students demand philosophers such as Plato and Kant are removed from syllabus because they are white

43 https://www.nus.org.uk/en/news/why-is-my-curriculum-white/

44 Oxford Uni must decolonise its campus and curriculum, say students

45 'Decolonising the curriculum': A conversation – CRASSH

46 The 'decolonise the curriculum' movement re-racialises knowledge

47 Delgado, R. and Stefancic, J. (2017) *Critical Race Theory* (3rd Edition) NYU Press.

48 Why are politicians suddenly talking about their 'lived experience'? I Kwame Anthony Appiah

49 Why are politicians suddenly talking about their 'lived experience'? I Kwame Anthony Appiah

50 https://www.theguardian.com/commentisfree/2020/nov/14/lived-experience-kamala-harris?fbclid=IwAR2igYyvqtP5EU8wAS7miHls8k-cVWlX4aGyIxaK-UJPA6DKu4eKbJCleO44

51 The Left's obsession with subjectivity

52 Ibram X Kendi, (2019) *How to be an antiracist*, Bodley Head.

53 Binna Kandola, (2018) Racism at Work, The danger of indifference, Pearn Kandola.

54 Delgado, R. and Stefancic, J. (2017) *Critical Race Theory* (3rd Edition) NYU Press.

55 Ibram X Kendi, (2019) *How to be an antiracist*, Bodley Head.

56 Reni Eddo-Lodge, (2017) *Why I'm no longer talking to white people about race*, Bloomsbury.

57 Robin DiAngelo, (2018) *White Fragility, Why it's so hard for white people to talk about race*, Penguin Random House.

58 Robin DiAngelo, (2018) *White Fragility, Why it's so hard for white people to talk about race*, Penguin Random House.

59 Robin DiAngelo, (2018) *White Fragility, Why it's so hard for white people to talk about race*, Penguin Random House.

60 https://www.civitas.org.uk/content/files/Disparity.pdf

61 Kemi Badenoch: The problem with critical race theory

62 https://nymag.com/intelligencer/2020/07/antiracism-training-white-fragility-robin-diangelo-ibram-kendi.html?fbclid=IwAR2UmwfpPeaYu5aOfcfeuDsF1ZPSWosi9HHvc7umPrXlsxI2l-tU_oGJQYZY

63 The Wages of Woke

64 Does Diversity Training Work the Way It's Supposed To?

65 Unconscious bias training alone will not stop discrimination, say critics

66 https://www.psychosisofwhiteness.com/

67 Does Diversity Training Work the Way It's Supposed To?

68 Unconscious bias training alone will not stop discrimination, say critics

69 Ibram X Kendi, (2019) *How to be an antiracist*, Bodley Head.

70 Lasch-Quinn, E. (2001) *Race Experts*. Rowman and Littlefield.

71 https://freebeacon.com/culture/the-wages-of-woke-2/

72 http://www.runnymedetrust.org/uploads/The%20School%20Report. pdf

73 https://www.ethnicity-facts-figures.service.gov.uk/education-skills-and-training/11-to-16-years-old/gcse-results-attainment-8-for-children-aged-14-to-16-key-stage-4/latest#by-ethnicity

74 https://www.civitas.org.uk/content/files/Disparity.pdf

75 http://www.runnymedetrust.org/uploads/The%20School%20Report. pdf

76 https://assets.publishing.service.gov.uk/government/uploads/system/uploads/attachment_data/file/807862/Timpson_review.pdf

77 How we think about disparity

78 https://www.runnymedetrust.org/projects-and-publications/education/the-school-report.html

79 The School That Tried to End Racism

80 https://johnmcwhorter.substack.com/p/more-on-what-modern-anti-racism-does

81 Kemi Badenoch: The problem with critical race theory

82 Degree attainment gaps

83 Institute for the Study of Civil Society The Racialisation of Campus Relations

84 N ove mber 2 0 2 0 un ive rsitie suk .ac .uk

85 Racism in universities is a systemic problem, not a series of incidents | Kehinde Andrews

86 https://www.universitiesuk.ac.uk/policy-and-analysis/reports/Documents/2020/tackling-racial-harassment-in-higher-education.pdf

87 Kandola, B. (2018) *Racism at Work*, Pearn Kandola Publishing.

88 Kandola, B. (2018) *Racism at Work*, Pearn Kandola Publishing.

89 How we think about disparity

90 BME workers far more likely to be trapped in insecure work, TUC analysis reveals

91 Diversity-Related Training: What Is It Good For? - Heterodox Academy

92 https://www.grovo.com/lessons/why-your-groups-diversity-is-an-asset

93 https://www.coursera.org/learn/diversity-inclusion-workplace

94 https://www.futurelearn.com/courses/diversity-inclusion-awareness

95 https://www.mslearning.microsoft.com/course/72169/launch

96 https://heterodoxacademy.org/blog/diversity-related-training-what-is-it-good-for/

97 https://heterodoxacademy.org/blog/diversity-related-training-what-is-it-good-for/

98 https://heterodoxacademy.org/blog/diversity-related-training-what-is-it-good-for/

99 https://www.activebystander.co.uk/how-to-intervene/

100 Reni Eddo-Lodge, (2017) *Why I'm no longer talking to white people about race*, Bloomsbury.

101 Robin DiAngelo, (2018) *White Fragility, Why it's so hard for white people to talk about race*, Penguin Random House.

102 Ibram X Kendi, (2019) *How to be an antiracist*, Bodley Head.

103 Delgado, R. and Stefancic, J. (2017) *Critical Race Theory* (3rd Edition) NYU Press.

104 https://www.theguardian.com/business/2021/feb/11/unconscious-bias-is-utter-crap-kpmg-staff-shock-uk-chair-zoom-comments-bill-michael

105 https://heterodoxacademy.org/blog/diversity-related-training-what-is-it-good-for/

106 https://www.mindingthecampus.org/2020/10/29/dont-go-for-woke-microaggressions-are-unscientific/

CIVITAS

Our Aims and Programmes

- We facilitate informed public debate by providing accurate factual information on the social issues of the day, publishing informed comment and analysis, and bringing together leading protagonists in open discussion. Civitas never takes a corporate view on any of the issues tackled during the course of this work. Our current focus is on issues such as education, health, crime, social security, manufacturing, the abuse of human rights law, and the European Union.

- We ensure that there is strong evidence for all our conclusions and present the evidence in a balanced and objective way. Our publications are usually refereed by independent commentators, who may be academics or experts in their field.

- We strive to benefit public debate through independent research, reasoned argument, lucid explanation and open discussion. We stand apart from party politics and transitory intellectual fashions.

- Uniquely among think tanks, we play an active, practical part in rebuilding civil society by running schools on Saturdays and after-school hours so that children who are falling behind at school can achieve their full potential.

Subscriptions and Membership

For subscriptions and membership forms, go to:
https://www.civitas.org.uk/subscriptions-and-membership/
or call (0)20 7799 6677

Book Subscriptions – £35 a year (UK only): If you would like to stay abreast of Civitas' latest work, you can have all of our books delivered to your door as soon as they are published.

Friends of Civitas – £25 special offer for the first year (UK only): As a Friend of Civitas you will receive all of our publications – including not only our books but all online releases – throughout the year.

Renewals for Existing Members: If you are an existing member who has previously paid via cheque or using our internal form but would like to renew with the ease and convenience of PayPal, please access the link above.

Make a Donation: If you like our work and would like to help see it continue, please consider making a donation.

Supporters of Civitas: If you would like to support our work on a rolling basis, there is a variety of advanced membership levels on offer.

Forms can be either faxed to
+44 (0)20 7799 6688 or posted to:

Civitas: Institute For The Study Of Civil Society
First Floor
55 Tufton Street
Westminster
London
SW1P 3QL.

Please make cheques payable to Civitas.
Email: subs@civitas.org.uk

Civitas is a registered charity, No. 1085494